The River Cottage

Game Handbook

The River Cottage Game Handbook

by Tim Maddams

with an introduction by
Hugh Fearnley-Whittingstall

rivercottage.net

BLOOMSBURY

For Isaac and Flora

Bloomsbury Publishing
An imprint of Bloomsbury Publishing Plc

50 Bedford Square
London
WC1B 3DP
UK

1385 Broadway
New York
NY 10018
USA

www.bloomsbury.com

BLOOMSBURY and the Diana logo are trademarks of Bloomsbury Publishing Plc

First published in Great Britain 2015

British Library Cataloguing-in-Publication Data
A catalogue record for this book is available from the British Library.

Library of Congress Cataloguing-in-Publication data has been applied for.

ISBN: 978-1-4088-5832-5

2 4 6 8 10 9 7 5 3 1

Project editor: Janet Illsley
Designer: Will Webb
Illustrator: Toby Atkins
Indexer: Hilary Bird

The publishers would also like to thank Sam Carlisle for his assistance.

Printed and bound in Italy by Graphicom

www.rivercottage.net

Contents

All meat used to be 'game'. Ten millennia ago, every ounce of animal protein consumed by humans was hungered for, hunted down, hard won. It wasn't until people began farming animals that a distinction could be drawn between wild and farmed meat. We bred our domesticated livestock over centuries to be fat, slow, succulent and, above all, abundant. One consequence of our success in this venture is that game now exists only on the fringes of our diets. Even the most committed and adventurous of carnivores is likely to eat far more farmed meat than wild. And in that process – the taming of our tastes, if you like – we have lost something.

We are so used to the pale, mild, well-fatted flesh of domesticated birds and beasts that game, dark and lean and richly flavoured, can come as a bit of a shock. What can also be shocking is that game so often arrives – back from a shoot, or on the butcher's counter, even sometimes at the table, too – looking like what it is: a dead animal. If you're used to chops, sausages, mince and chicken breasts, it's an eye-opener to behold a row of pigeons in their shiny grey feathers, or a muddy-furred rabbit, as the raw ingredient of your dinner; or indeed to be presented with that rabbit roasted on your plate – skinned and headless, but with its limbs and distinctive body shape still much in evidence.

For some, this is a real problem. Many consumers are comfortable only with food that is designed and controlled by the hand of man and sanitised, if not outright disguised, before it reaches the table. In fact, for many, the higher the level of intervention, the more processing and polishing involved, the greater the trust placed in the food. But for some of us, the opposite is the case. With meat, in particular, the less it has been interfered with, both during its life and after its death, the better. I count myself in this camp, and so does Tim Maddams.

Anyone who loves meat, and has no ethical objections to eating it per se, will still come up against all kinds of problems when buying it in practice. The poorest levels of animal welfare are still represented on our shop shelves – in factory-farmed pork, for instance. And even if you stride firmly to the opposing end of the spectrum and choose organic meat raised in the highest welfare systems, you can't deny that those animals have still lived lives hedged and hemmed in by humans. Wild game (but not reared game) offers an alternative because it is plucked from the midst of a natural, instinctive existence. It would be disingenuous to say that we don't still shape the environment of those creatures to some extent, either deliberately or otherwise, but wild game animals and birds live in a state of freedom that farmed animals can never achieve.

That is just one reason why I like game meat and why I would like to see it better understood and more widely consumed in the UK. We can nourish ourselves perfectly well without meat if we choose to do so, but if we are to end an animal's life in order to satisfy our hunger, surely snatching that animal in a split second from a natural existence is about the best and most humane way to do it.

There are many other reasons to celebrate game, not least the fact that it offers a broad and varied range of delicious tastes and textures. Animals that have grown on a truly wild diet have flesh imbued with all sorts of herby, rich, sweet and pungent flavours. The leanness of game is hugely appealing in a world where our diets are dominated by fat and sugar. And there are the benefits of higher omega-3 levels in creatures that have eaten a diet rich in grass and greens, as opposed to grains.

As with any meat, game does not come without a side order of thorny issues. The quick, clean dispatch of an animal or bird in the wild cannot always be guaranteed, for instance. And there is the knotty problem of game that is not truly wild – the pheasants and partridges that are fed and fattened by gamekeepers so that they may be driven deliberately over waiting guns. Is this better than being raised in a farmyard and trucked to an abattoir? In the end you must make up your own mind about this, and the other ethical issues relating to game. In this book Tim offers you the information you will need to do so, alongside his own frank opinions on the matter. He does not shy away from the complex questions that surround meat-eating in general, and game-eating in particular, and I admire his honest and thoughtful writing on the subject.

I've had the great pleasure to work with Tim in the kitchen, but also to shoot and fish with him. His infectious enthusiasm and energy are coupled with some fiercely held principles: he's someone who takes his food, its provenance and its welfare, very seriously indeed. He has that quality so many good hunters share: a genuine fascination with, and respect for, the prey animal. And, for Tim, that fascination and respect extend into the kitchen.

He has a wonderful knack for enhancing and augmenting game meats in a way that emphasises their inherently rich, wild qualities. Tim's recipes will tempt you to the butcher's, if not the local gunsmith's, and have you cooking up seared pigeon with blackberries and mushrooms, or slow-roast spiced wild duck, before you know it. When you do, you will begin to understand just what a joy it can be to eat meat from creatures that have lived a wild, or at least a semi-wild, existence. If cooked well – and Tim tells you all you need to know on that front – it tastes fantastic. But the knowledge that the animal you are eating has lived well too is about the best seasoning you could ask for.

Hugh Fearnley-Whittingstall, East Devon, July 2015

Starting Out

I remember the first time I ate game. It was a very significant

event, a turning point that was to shape my life and my career. I had just turned seven and my mum was given a hare by a local farmer. I remember the stink of the guts as she cleaned out the animal, the crackle of the sinews as she removed the skin and the high, gamey aroma of the meat, which was slowly transformed into a savoury delight during an afternoon of slow cooking. And I remember the astonishing flavour of the stew. I was hooked, and there was no going back.

I still love game for its deliciousness, its wonderful range of flavours. It is the most intense, delicate, rich and varied meat there is and, when you get to grips with the techniques and skills required to cook it, it will take you on a culinary journey that no other food can.

But game has become more than an exceptionally tasty food to me. It represents a well-informed, compassionate, intelligent way of eating that is often lacking in our lives today. Preparing, cooking and eating wild meat is one way to forge a closer link with, and a deeper understanding of, the food on our plates.

Because of this, I want to share what I've learned about the whole process of obtaining, assessing, preparing and eating wild meat. And I want to accompany you on a journey – out of the safe, clean confines of the butcher's shop or the supermarket and into the unfamiliar world of whole dead animals. I'll show you how to deal with them and how to use them safely to feed yourself, your friends and your family.

I have written this book not so much for experienced wild meat enthusiasts (though I hope you'll pick it up and enjoy it if you are one) as for the conscientious home cook who is occasionally offered a haunch of venison, or even a whole carcass, a brace of pheasants or the odd duck or rabbit, and is keen to accept this generous offer but has no idea where to start preparing such a gift. I intend to guide you and to offer you some insight from the point of view of a chef – but also as a practical man with a family to feed.

Even for the most enthusiastic and experienced of cooks, dealing with meat that was, very obviously, a living creature only a short time ago can be daunting. For most of us, it's outside our daily experience of food. So think of this book as a basic tool kit for dealing with that situation. You'll be doing the work, of course, but the book will be on hand to pass you the right tools, at the right moments, and ease the process along.

I will, of course, be discussing the various ways that wild meat is harvested, and making a few serious ethical points. But my main aim is to change the place of game on your menu from the occasional to the everyday and encourage you to release your kitchen creativity and enjoy some new culinary experiences. In short, I want to get you eating more wild meat and giving it a regular place on your supper table.

A brace of pheasants

What is game?

'Game' is simply any wild animal or bird hunted for food or sport, and/or the meat of these creatures. Actually, if you look at an encyclopedia or on the internet, you will learn that in this country 'game' is also a legal term for a short and specific list of wild animals and birds. Defined by the Game Act of 1831, it lists only grouse, partridge, hare, pheasant and ptarmigan. I refer to these as 'true game'.

In this book, however, I'm concerned with the much wider gamut of wild meat, taking in creatures such as deer, wildfowl, ducks and waders, and 'vermin' such as rabbits, rooks and squirrels. These are animals that have, over centuries, proven to be delicious and useful sources of protein, whether they are shot for recreation or as a means of controlling natural populations.

The notion of shooting or hunting as 'recreation' or 'sport' is difficult for some, but there is no point in trying to avoid it. The word 'sport' has been used for centuries to describe the hunting and shooting of game, and it recognises the fact that pursuing game is a test of skill which many, myself included, actively enjoy – especially when we are successful. For some the sporting, and indeed social aspects of shooting, take precedence over the eating of the meat. For me the two are always connected. I never go shooting without thinking about what I might bring home, and how I might cook it.

But whether you want to go shooting or not, if you like cooking, it's worth remembering that game is a versatile and under-celebrated part of our food culture. High in nutrients and low in fat, it is a healthy choice too. Learning more about game and its possibilities in the kitchen will open up a whole new world of culinary experience for you. It's a big step outside the safe confines of normal cookery, but it is really not that complicated. Animals are mostly similar in shape – and birds also follow the same basic design – so once you learn to work with one game species you'll be able to tackle the others.

Game is food for the body and the mind. Nowadays, for the most part, we are far removed from the process of slaughter and butchery that delivers our meat. Hunting your own game is the perfect way to understand and accept these processes outside the abattoir. Game can connect you with the past and change the future of the way you eat. It will influence the way you look at all other meats and teach you new and useful skills. And, not least, it will make you a better cook and reward you with some of the finest food on the planet.

True game

Though it does vary in different places and at different times of the year, the term true game is restricted to the following wild animals and birds, which are killed for sport and/or food during specified seasons.

A brace of rabbits

- Common pheasant
- Red-legged partridge
- Grey partridge
- Red grouse

- Mountain hare
- Brown hare
- Black grouse (currently not shot)
- Ptarmigan (currently rarely shot)

Vermin

The following species are technically 'vermin', i.e. animals considered to be pests or a nuisance. They are not protected by any specific closed seasons. There are many old countryside rules applied to the taking of these creatures but, more often than not these days, they are killed almost as a matter of course. This is often as a result of pressure from landowners and farmers whose valuable crops are seen as an abundant supper table by these creatures.

- Rook
- Wood pigeon
- Rabbit

- Grey squirrel
- Wild boar

Wildfowl

I have split the birds described as wildfowl into smaller groups. I have also left out the species that are currently protected for conservation reasons, as you're unlikely to be cooking any of these in the near future.

Ducks
- Mallard
- Teal
- Wigeon
- Pochard
- Pin tail
- Gadwall

Waders
- Woodcock
- Snipe

Geese
- Canada
- Greylag
- Pink-footed

Deer

The species listed below are all living wild in the UK and, of course, the term we use for the meat of this group of animals is venison. Not all of the deer living wild or being farmed in the UK are indigenous species, but all have made the UK their home to a greater or lesser extent and are a fascinating and beautiful part of our countryside.

- Red deer
- Fallow deer
- Sika deer

- Roe deer
- Muntjac
- Chinese water deer

Why I hunt game

Humans have been eating wild meat for a very long time. Although we don't need it in order to survive, or be healthy, and our ability to forage plants and fungi has also had an important role to play, our ability to use tools and employ cunning to kill prey has shaped our evolution, making us the way we are today.

I am a hunter. I shoot wood pigeons, pheasants, ducks, geese, rabbits, deer and the occasional squirrel, rook or partridge. I am also a committed ethical foodie. I believe that we should eat less meat and more veg, farm organically, look after the fish stocks of the world and live in as sustainable a way as we can. For me, hunting is not at odds with my ethical approach – on the contrary, it is a very important element of it.

This is in part because I believe a wild animal will have lived life as nature intended. These creatures spend their time eating, resting and reproducing; their lives are natural and normal, they have freedom to roam more or less where they like. If hunted, their deaths are usually clean and swift (and they also have a good chance of getting away completely unharmed). Inevitably, sometimes, birds and animals will be wounded rather than killed outright. While this cannot be completely avoided, all experienced and responsible hunters use a dog to quickly retrieve or track the wounded animal for immediate humane dispatch. I, for one, would still choose a wild rabbit over an intensively farmed pig any day of the week. I would far rather be responsible for the death of a wild animal than for the poor standard of living that some farm animals must endure.

I believe that shooting and preparing game fosters a deep regard for animals that, for the most part, is lacking in today's food culture. We have founded several generations who have no idea where their meat comes from, or the conditions in which it was reared. Eating game is one way to re-establish this connection because inherent in game cookery is an understanding of the simple facts of life and death. It's a pretty unusual person who can gut, skin, prepare and cook a whole animal without developing a healthy respect for it and an understanding of where it comes from and what it's worth – more so if you've hunted and killed the creature too.

Of course, the amount of game we might be able to harvest could not hope to fulfil our current demand for meat. But is that such a bad thing? We consume far too much animal flesh: eating less, and making sure some of what we eat is wild, can surely only be good for us and for the environment.

I celebrate the fact that I can – and often do – provide the meat that goes on my table, and I enjoy hunting on many levels. A hunting trip is a deeply satisfying break from the hustle and bustle of everyday life, much like a fishing or a foraging trip. I enjoy both the solitary hours and the time spent with good friends. There is a deep and refreshing appreciation of the world around me when I go shooting,

and a feeling of pride that comes with the ability to dispatch a wood pigeon or pheasant cleanly and efficiently when the chance comes my way. I am astounded again and again by the beauty of these animals and their ability to surprise me, and being in the field makes me feel connected to the world in a new way. There can be little doubt that the act of killing animals for food does satisfy an ancient and emotional need within the hunter.

While it's undeniable that making a kill stirs up strong feelings, after a short time that emotion is replaced by a sense of anticipation, of looking forward to the meal that this animal or bird will provide for the table.

In addition to game shot for sport, there will always be meat that has been produced as a result of pest control – rabbits, pigeons and rooks, for example. Not to eat these animals is simply wasteful. Refusing to eat lamb might mean that less lamb was sold and fewer animals were raised and slaughtered. The demand affects the supply. However, if we are talking about wild rooks and pigeons shot to protect crops or deer culled in order to maintain a healthy population, then refusing to eat the meat will have no effect on the number of animals being killed or reared in the future. We might as well enjoy them.

Wild and reared game

Many game species are truly wild but others are bred and reared in a controlled way, making them a rather different proposition from an ethical point of view. Highlighting some of the conservation issues around wild species, and outlining the main processes involved in rearing will, I hope, help you decide which game species you can feel happy about making a meal of.

Wild game

Deer are usually wild (or they are kept as part of a park herd and are therefore semi-wild) and, as there are no natural predators of deer in this country, their numbers must be controlled to maintain a healthy herd. The happy result of this control process is venison.

In most cases, the deer destined to be shot will have no idea what is about to happen to it, and there is a strong argument for wild venison being one of the most ethical meats available. It is rare for a deer to be wounded by a stalker unless, as occasionally happens, something goes amiss. There's always the odd incident where a shot goes slightly astray, or an animal moves at the critical moment and, in this case, the animal must be traced and humanely dispatched as quickly as possible.

For similar reasons, I also feel comfortable eating rabbit, pigeon, grey squirrel, geese, wildfowl, hare and rooks. They, too, are wild and live a very natural life.

A brace of red grouse

With the exception of some wildfowl and hare, which are simply shot because they taste so good and are not a conservation concern, they are killed because they are a threat to agriculture and forestry or, in the case of squirrels, indigenous species. It makes sense to kill them in a way that leaves the meat safe for consumption. Often a shotgun is used, with the increased chance of injury rather than swift death. Trained dogs are a key part of shotgun hunting, not just for finding lost birds or animals, but also for collecting any wounded prey quickly, for humane dispatch. Rabbits are usually rifle shot, often at night using a lamp.

Truly wild game is, of course, left to its own devices in its natural habitat up until the point of dispatch. However, that doesn't mean that wild shooting can't affect an ecosystem. Making a huge dent in the numbers of one particular creature could have an impact. That is why conservation and careful management of wild shooting are so important.

Reared game

Not all the animals we regard as game are truly wild and the system of rearing and releasing birds for large-scale shooting can raise difficult ethical questions. Pheasants, partridges and some mallard ducks are bred in large numbers, raised and released purely so they can be killed by people with guns who enjoy going out into the countryside to shoot them; the fact that the end product is food is not the main reason that this happens.

I've visited game-rearing sheds and spoken to many experts, and I have seen exceptionally good systems for rearing birds on both small and large scales. However, it's inevitable that when many birds are reared together in an enclosed space – especially species that are not really domesticated – they will experience some level of stress before their release in the woods. More can be done to ensure better welfare for these animals. One way forward is tighter legislation, and many of us who shoot support this approach.

Birds reared for shooting fall between two categories: they are not classed as agricultural animals (although they are most certainly farmed), so they are not covered by agricultural legislation. Nor are they classed as wild animals, because they clearly are not until they have been released and had a chance to naturalise to some extent, so they are not covered by any of the wild bird legislation either. The good news is that, in 2010, the Code of Practice for the Welfare of Gamebirds Reared for Sporting Purposes was drawn up in partnership between the government and the Game Farmers' Association (GFA). Although this is not, in itself, law, it can be used as the basis for prosecution under the Animal Welfare Act 2006.

Another way to improve the situation is through better shoot management. People who like to shoot don't always have ready access to land on which to do it and so they will spend their hard-earned money, often a lot of it, on a day's driven shooting. It's big business. But there are cases where too many birds are shot. The birds then flood the market, making them of very little value, and this has led to birds being buried rather than sold – and eaten. There can be no excuse for this kind of behaviour. Shoots that offer 'big bag' days must ensure they have a market for the birds, even if they give them away. They must not be wasted.

There are environmental pros and cons to rearing game. On the down side, reared game needs to eat a lot of feed: we expend fuel and other resources to raise these birds. A fair amount of carbon is produced per pheasant (slightly higher than that produced for a farmed chicken, apparently).

To produce good quantities of a specific species – and protect them – you must control their predators and parasites. A gamekeeper deals with the latter using drugs, in much the same way as a farmer would worm livestock. This has little impact on the environment. Dealing with predators, however, creates a secondary harvest – and not an edible one. Many foxes and mink are trapped, snared or shot each year because they pose a threat to game birds. Predator control like this is one reason that people object to shooting – why, after all, shouldn't foxes be allowed to take a few partridge? They are only doing what comes naturally to them. The problem, of course, is that you would soon end up with many more foxes and very few partridges. What we have at present is, arguably, a kind of equilibrium: the many birds being reared for shooting are an important food source for a healthy – albeit controlled – population of foxes.

But there is a strong argument for the importance of shooting to the conservation of our countryside. A lot of the diverse and semi-wild habitat in the UK is there, in part, to facilitate the release and shooting of game birds: these places exist because the land has greater value to the landowner as game cover than it does as wheat fields. Without shooting, large areas of woodland, moorland and wetlands could disappear (unless another profitable use could be found for them).

In addition, land managed for the shooting of game will always have a higher biodiversity than land used for farming crops or animals and, with the exception of predators as mentioned above, this biodiversity is encouraged and allowed to flourish. The British Association for Shooting and Conservation (BASC) claims that shooters contribute to conservation and biodiversity on around two-thirds of the rural landmass in the UK.

Whenever people express a dislike for shooting it is often large-scale commercial shoots that they are focused on and it's easy to see why. Hundreds of birds being shot by a few people paying hundreds of pounds for the privilege seems elitist and has little to do with feeding your family. But large shoots, while they have their faults, are good for the rural economy and tourism, providing jobs and money in areas where there may not be many alternatives. According to BASC, shooting and shooting-related activities are worth millions of pounds a year to the UK economy.

It's up to you to choose the game you eat. It's tempting to try and stick only to truly wild species and leave the semi-farmed, semi-wild birds alone, but there's no escaping the fact that these are the very birds that will be most easily and commonly available and shot in the largest numbers. It wouldn't be right either to let all that meat go to waste. On balance, I would still rather eat a reared pheasant or partridge than almost any farmed chicken, with properly free-range and organic chickens being the exception. To cautiously draw a comparison, I would say that while a pheasant, mallard or partridge is being reared, it experiences a level of welfare and environmental enrichment equivalent to that of a standard free-range chicken. Once released, I would say its level of welfare is far higher.

I do eat pheasant and partridge. But I base my game cookery around a whole panoply of wild game. I hope that, one day, fewer birds will be reared for shooting. But the demands for big 'bags' will only drop when more hunters measure the value of their sport not in terms of sheer numbers, but in the diversity of what is offered, and even the conservation status of the land they are shooting on.

Conservation

Sustainability is a word that gets bandied about a lot these days, but it's a crucial thing to consider when we look at the way we consume food (and the energy needed to produce it). It's as relevant to game as to any other ingredient.

The first consideration is the fairly obvious one that we must not take so many animals from an ecosystem as to cause irreparable damage to that species. For example, if we shoot too many wild teal or woodcock, we run the risk of causing a total dearth of those birds, which clearly is in nobody's interest – least of all that of the teal or woodcock. Likewise, we shouldn't try to *increase* the numbers of a specific species too much, as this can adversely affect closely associated members of that ecosystem.

The second consideration is more subtle and harder to define. We must go about the practice of harvesting game (and rearing it, controlling its predators and managing its environment) in a way that maintains the safe balance of the ecosystem while ensuring a surplus of 'output' to siphon off and use as food.

Whether the population of a certain species is under threat is not always evident. For example, there may be a high concentration of a certain species in one area because it is a particularly good habitat for them. This might make them appear to be abundant, but the national (or international) picture may be very different. Conversely, a very small number of wood pigeons living in a particular spot does not reflect the fact that nationally they are on the increase, despite huge numbers being shot each year.

The main issue surrounding conservation of wild game is that there is no national record kept of animals culled. Game clubs, quite rightly, keep records of how many animals and birds are killed each year, but these are not always collected together and analysed to give the bigger picture.

The British Association for Shooting and Conservation (BASC), the Game and Wildlife Conservation Trust (GWCT) and others are working hard to gather as much information as possible throughout the UK each year to improve our understanding and the British Deer Society (BDS) periodically releases survey results, which provide a national overview of the location of the different deer species and an estimate of their numbers. It is only through the hard work of these groups and through collaboration with conservation groups outside the world of shooting and hunting that we can gain a better understanding of conservation in game. In most cases, it is best to err on the side of caution until the picture becomes clearer.

I have compiled a conservation grading system and applied it to every species covered in this book, to give an indication of their conservation status. The grading system cannot be perfect as there are significant variables involved, not least the local abundance of a species which is considered to be in decline elsewhere. To complicate matters further, numbers of reared and released birds may be swelling but they often don't breed well in the wild so won't necessarily boost a struggling local population. Migrating birds also have a temporary impact on numbers.

- Abundant population Hunting has a low impact on species.

- Migratory or fluctuating population Should be hunted in moderation, with strict bag limits, and eaten less often (unlikely to be a problem as these species are only rarely offered for sale).

- Population fluctuating or declining Should only be taken/eaten very rarely and from locally abundant sources.

- Species under threat Or not enough reliable information available – don't eat.

There is far greater cooperation these days between conservation groups, managers and landowners. As this continues to improve, we will see an even greater level of biodiversity on moors, woodlands and downlands that are managed for shooting. In the past, for example, many birds of prey were killed and their habitat destroyed to keep the numbers of game birds high. But this practice is now illegal and more enlightened gamekeeping will ensure that the numbers of apex predators such as hen harriers and golden eagles can grow.

Hunting & Shooting

Those who shoot wild animals for food, myself included, have a habit of expecting others to know what is involved. But, of course, those who don't hunt usually have only a vague understanding of what actually happens. So here are a few facts about the mechanics of it all.

Game in this country is taken either by 'stalking' (the act of locating game and dispatching it with a shot from a rifle), or by shooting (the act of firing a shotgun at game in flight). Falcons and other raptors are also trained for hunting, but this happens on a far smaller scale than shooting.

Stalking

Stalking usually refers to hunting deer in the wild. Generally, a deerstalker is a lone, trained hunter, who has achieved a qualification in deer law and safe game meat processing. It can involve anything from a long and unpleasant crawl along a stream bed to get into position, to simply sitting in a high seat and awaiting a suitable animal to cull. Deer are almost always shot with a high-powered rifle, except in special circumstances when they may be taken with specially prepared shotgun loads (legal permission must be sought first).

Stalking actually refers to the process of getting close enough to your prey to dispatch it with a clean shot. This could be from an air rifle, a small-bore rifle or a full-bore rifle, depending on the prey. It could even mean using a camera or a pair of binoculars, should you simply wish to observe the animal's behaviour. For instance, you may well practise stalking when sneaking up on a few rooks in the tree with an air rifle: it's no less of a stalk simply because there are no deer involved.

Shooting

Shooting means taking birds or small animals for the pot with a shotgun. The prey might be anything from a few wood pigeons to a hundred pheasants and there are several forms of shooting. The hunters who shoot are often referred to as 'guns'.

A gamekeeper and their team take care of everything from habitat management and bird-rearing to controlling pests and predators. They also organise shoot days and look after the hunters. Beaters are the people who 'flush' game from cover, often with the aid of well-trained dogs. They walk through woods, or other ground cover, beating their sticks on trees and generally making a noise. The job is sometimes perceived to be straightforward, but managing a team of beaters in thick cover to ensure the best chance of a successful flush is no easy task. Traversing rough ground, farmland and woodland is physically demanding too.

Rough shooting or walked-up shooting

This is an informal gathering of a few hunters, or guns, a few dogs and a gamekeeper. It will usually involve a lot of walking and dog work, in order to present a few birds and rabbits to the hunters, offering them a challenging shot. As shown in the example illustrated below, the hunters walk in a line with the dogs just in front through game cover of some kind, or possibly just along a hedge or through a wood. The dogs will locate and flush game birds or animals from the cover and the hunters will take a shot if it is safe to do so. A small number of birds or animals dead at the end of the day is the expected result.

This is a relatively challenging type of shooting as the hunter must be aware at all times of where everyone else and their dogs are positioned, and is often called upon to take a very quick shot.

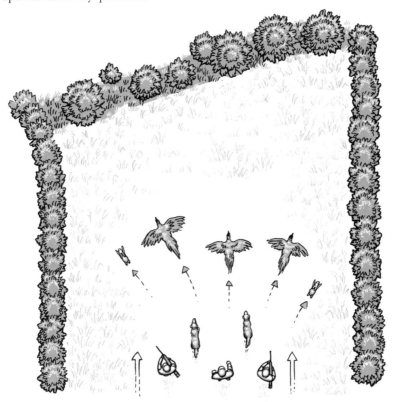

The dogs flush the game, working close to the line of guns as they walk up the cover; the dogs then retrieve any game the guns have shot.

Decoying

This is the practice of luring wild birds within range of a gun for a humane shot, by way of placing imitation or dead birds in front of a hidden hunter. The idea is that birds will see the decoys and come over to have a closer look or be encouraged into landing. It's not as easy as it sounds. Good pigeon hunters, for example, must constantly observe their fields, learning where will give the best chance of a good day's shooting. Simply throwing down a few decoys and sitting in the hedge with a gun will not usually do the trick; you need to understand the behaviour patterns of the birds involved to have any hope of success. Wood pigeons prefer to fly into the wind, so wind direction is useful in working out the best way to set up the decoys in relation to the position of the hide.

Incidentally, this is the modern meaning of 'decoy'. In the past, the term was actually applied to man-made ponds and lakes, surrounded by woodland, designed to attract wildfowl. Birds were then trapped in various ways.

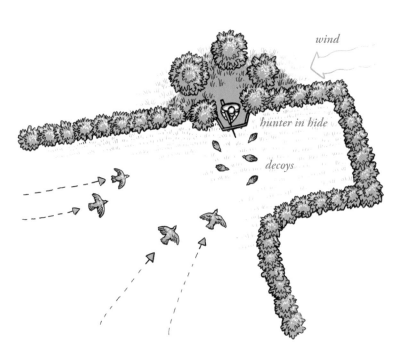

wind

hunter in hide

decoys

Pigeon decoying: the flocking instinct of the pigeons attracts them to the decoys and within range of the hidden hunter.

Flighting

This is the act of working out or observing flight lines, or roost destinations, of birds such as wood pigeons or wild ducks. Hunters may use a few decoys to slow the birds, or give them confidence to come close or land, but the destination is home, where the birds were heading anyway. This type of shooting can be extremely challenging, particularly with ducks, as they tend to fly in the half-light of dawn and dusk. As dusk approaches, for example, they suddenly take flight and head for their home pond, where they will spend the night safely floating on the water. Hunters conceal themselves in a hide and wait for the flight to begin. As you can imagine, shooting at ducks in the twilight as they suddenly appear out of nowhere is not at all easy, and I believe it's this challenge, along with the full flavour of the meat, that makes wild ducks one of the most sought-after quarry species.

Technically, the term 'flighting' refers to the act of shooting birds in this way, but the word is often used to describe birds in flight, as in 'look at that flight of pigeons coming into the wood'.

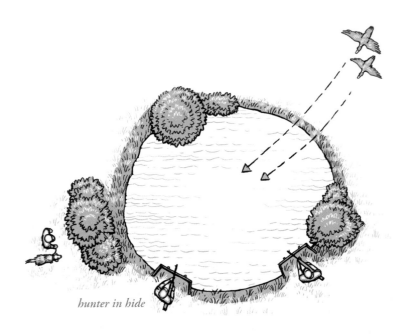

hunter in hide

A duck flight: hidden hunters effectively ambush ducks returning to their water; a dog and picker-up wait to collect the birds.

Beaters at the end of a shoot

Driven shooting

This is what most people imagine when they think of shooting. Guns (hunters) are lined up in a predetermined place, each taking a specific point known as a 'peg'. Pegs are often shared out between hunters in a random way – the guns will select a card with their peg number on it at random from a fan of cards. Guns will then move up a peg or two on each new drive, so that everyone gets a peg in the middle of the line at least once in the day, making the sharing of the shooting fair. Once the guns are in place, a team of beaters then drives the birds from cover over the waiting guns. This cover may be woodland or moorland, or it could be a crop of some kind planted specifically for the purpose, typically maize, kale or mustard; these are known as cover crops. Often the birds will have been reared and released for the purpose of shooting. This form of shooting takes some of the element of uncertainty out of the day and is relatively straightforward and predictable, making it very popular.

beaters

waiting guns

The beaters work as a team to flush birds over the guns during a game drive.

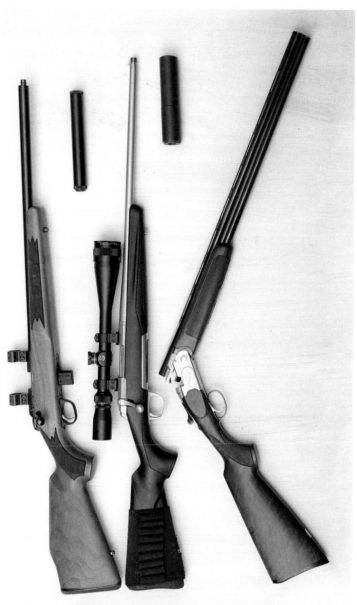

Left to right: .22 rimfire rifle and sound moderator;
.243 centre-fire rifle and sound moderator; 20-bore shotgun

Types of gun

As with all tools, you need the right gun for the job. The two basic types are rifles and shotguns. Both have different uses and each has variations suited to certain situations. For example, you wouldn't use the same rifle to shoot a rabbit as you would a deer. Safe conduct is the priority with any firearm and care must be taken at all times. I highly recommend some expert training from a reputable organisation before you start to use any gun on your own (see the Directory pp.248–9).

Rifle

A rifle gets its name from its rifled barrels – the inside of the barrel is marked with regular grooves which cause the bullet, propelled from a cartridge, to spin. This spinning motion increases the range and accuracy of the bullet, making a rifle by far the best method of killing prey at distances over 45 metres (50 yards.) With deer, it's also the only way of doing the job humanely and ensuring as far as possible a clean and, above all, safe shot. In order to own a rifle you will require a firearms certificate, issued by the local police authority.

Shotgun

A shotgun is a smooth-bore gun (as opposed to a 'rifled' gun, see above), either with single or double barrels. It fires shot (small metal pellets), which is contained in cartridges, along with wadding and powder. The cartridges are placed into the chamber (the top of the barrel) of the gun. With a semi-automatic, the cartridges go into a magazine: a device for automatically loading cartridges into the chamber.

When the gun is triggered, a single cartridge fires a certain amount of shot from the barrel of the gun. Only a small quantity of shot is released, often around 30g (1oz), and it travels like a comet with a tail, rather than spreading out to make a ball. This concentrates the shot into a small area where it can be most effective. The main reason that shot is used is for safety. If you fire a single piece of lead up in the sky and you miss your target, that piece of lead will have to come back down, and there's a very good chance of it killing someone. Shot falling from the sky, on the other hand, just feels like getting rained on. Shot also causes less damage to the fragile carcasses of birds in flight.

Different sizes and types of shot are available for different types of prey. These are denoted by a sizing system: the larger the number, the smaller the shot inside the cartridge. For example, 3 or 4 shot is fine for a goose but 5 or 6 shot would be better for pheasant and pigeon. Smaller shot sizes are typically used for clay target shooting. Cartridges are also available in different-sized loads and this refers to the weight of the shot inside the cartridge. The heavier the load, the more shot within the cartridge and so the more propellant will be used to achieve the correct velocity.

Shotgun cartridges, one opened to show contents

.22 rimfire rounds, soft-nosed (for use on rabbits, hare etc.)

Centre-fire rounds, expanding ammunition (for use on deer)

Hence, recoil will be more noticeable with heavier loads of shot. To own a shotgun you need to have a shotgun certificate issued to you by your police authority.

Picking up

This is the term used to describe the task of handlers and their trained dogs whose job it is to collect fallen prey and chase up wounded birds or animals. No organised shoot would allow shooting to take place without the aid of trained dogs and no hunter should ever go out without a good dog either.

Ferreting

Ferreting is the act of flushing rabbits from their warren by introducing a ferret down the hole. The rabbits will then bolt from the warren into the path of a waiting hunter with a shotgun, or they will be trapped in a net and dispatched with a swift blow from a priest to the head. This is an effective method of controlling rabbit and produces undamaged meat for the kitchen if the rabbits are not shot.

Non-toxic shot

The shooting of any ducks, geese, moorhens or coots in England, Wales and Northern Ireland must be done with non-toxic shot, i.e. not lead. Also non-toxic shot must be used for any species shot within a specifically identified Site of Special Scientific Interest (SSSI) and on the foreshore. This is due to concerns that an excess of lead shot could enter the watercourse and poison people and animals. In Scotland, there are slightly different rules requiring the use of non-toxic shot over wetlands for all species, but waterfowl can be shot with lead inland. This is a hotly debated subject amongst shooters because lead has better ballistic qualities than cheaper, non-toxic steel. There are better options than steel, but they cost more.

Lead in game

Most game birds (excluding wildfowl) are dispatched with lead shot. As this may result in traces of lead in the meat, young children, pregnant women and anyone with heart or liver problems should limit their consumption of shot game to once or twice a week at most. Cooking shot game in highly acidic sauces may encourage the lead to break down and possibly cause more of an issue. As non-toxic alternatives become more cost-effective, it seems likely that lead shot will be used less frequently.

In most parts of the country ducks, geese and other waterfowl must be shot with non-toxic shot, to protect the aquatic environment. The most common alternative to lead is steel. This won't harm you if digested, but it could break a tooth if you were to bite on it, so remove as much shot as possible from wildfowl before cooking. Large game such as deer and wild boar are unlikely to contain any lead. Usually the bullet will have left the body and all bullet-damaged meat should be removed.

A mature fallow buck

Game seasons

Not all game meat is available all year round. There is a complex and occasionally mystifying set of laws that govern the killing of various species at different times of the year. The time of year that a particular animal can be killed is called the 'open season' and conversely the time when it is protected is known as the 'closed season'. For example, the partridge open season runs from 1st September until 1st February. The tables on pp.38–43 show which animals are in season and when, in England, Wales, Scotland and Northern Ireland.

The main reason for open and closed seasons is to protect the breeding cycle. For example, no wild ducks are shot in the spring or summer when they are breeding to enable them to reproduce without the pressure of hunting. This also helps to ensure there will be more ducks to hunt next year. With ducks and geese, there are further complications. For example, the season for wild ducks in England and Wales runs from 1st September to 31st January, but this does not include the 'foreshore', where the season extends to 20th February. The foreshore is described as the strip of land below the high-tide mark of a normal tide. A normal tide is measured as the tide line occurring halfway between a spring and a neap tide.

As well as closed seasons, for some game species there are daylight restrictions. For example, without special permission from Natural England and a licence from the Department for the Environment, Food and Rural Affairs (DEFRA), it is illegal to shoot deer at night, the legal definition of night in this instance being 'the period between one hour after sunset and one hour before sunrise'. No game birds may be shot at night either, but the same does not apply to ducks, which may be shot at flight well past one hour after sunset.

The group of animals known as 'vermin' do not have a closed season. Animals such as these are not totally unprotected, as all wild animals are protected under the Wildlife and Countryside Act 1981 unless there is a general licence issued for the protection of agricultural crops, forestry etc. (or they are covered by other legislation). Hunters do not need to apply for a general licence (see p.68), though there may well be terms that need to be met before 'fatal control of a species is put into practice', for example you may be required to prove that you have attempted to scare pigeons off a crop before shooting can take place.

The open and closed season schedule for the various deer species is the most complex, as the seasons differ from one species to another. Also, the season for males and females is different, to protect the reproductive cycle and the future of the herd, and to allow more selective culling. For example, young male deer often have single spiked antlers. Known as spikers or prickets, they are very likely to injure older, more dominant males during the rut so these deer are often culled to prevent serious injury and protect the stronger genetics of the dominant male.

Open and closed seasons in England and Wales

TRUE GAME	JAN	FEB	MAR	APR	MAY
Common pheasant		plus 1st			'
Red-legged partridge		plus 1st			
Grey partridge		plus 1st			
Red grouse					
Black grouse					
Brown hare					
WILDFOWL					
Woodcock					
Snipe					
Mallard, inland					
Mallard, foreshore		until 20th			
Teal, inland					
Teal, foreshore		until 20th			
Wigeon, inland					
Wigeon, foreshore		until 20th			
Canada goose					
Greylag goose, inland					
Greylag goose, foreshore		until 20th			
Pink-footed goose, inland					
Pink-footed goose, foreshore		until 20th			
Golden plover					
Coot and moorhen					
DEER					
Red deer, male					
Red deer, female					
Fallow deer, male					
Fallow deer, female					
Sika deer, male					
Sika deer, female					
Roe deer, male					
Roe deer, female					
Muntjac deer, both sexes					
Chinese water deer, male					
Chinese water deer, female					

JUNE	JULY	AUG	SEPT	OCT	NOV	DEC
		from 12th				until 10th
		from 20th				until 10th
		from 12th				

Open and closed seasons in Scotland

TRUE GAME	JAN	FEB	MAR	APR	MAY
Common pheasant		plus 1st			
Red-legged partridge		plus 1st			
Grey partridge		plus 1st			
Red grouse					
Black grouse					
Ptarmigan					
Mountain hare					
Brown hare					
WILDFOWL					
Woodcock					
Snipe					
Mallard, inland					
Mallard, foreshore		until 20th			
Teal, inland					
Teal, foreshore		until 20th			
Wigeon, inland					
Wigeon, foreshore		until 20th			
Canada goose					
Greylag goose, inland					
Greylag goose, foreshore		until 20th			
Pink-footed goose, inland					
Pink-footed goose, foreshore		until 20th			
Golden plover					
Coot and moorhen					
DEER					
Red deer, male					
Red deer, female		until 15th			
Fallow deer, male					
Fallow deer, female		until 15th			
Sika deer, male					
Sika deer, female		until 15th			
Roe deer, male					
Roe deer, female					
Muntjac deer, both sexes					

	Open		Closed

JUNE	JULY	AUG	SEPT	OCT	NOV	DEC
				Open	Open	Open
			Open	Open	Open	Open
		Open	Open	Open	Open	Open
		from 12th	Open	Open	Open	until 10th
		from 20th	Open	Open	Open	until 10th
		from 12th	Open	Open	Open	until 10th
		Open	Open	Open	Open	
			Open	Open	Open	
				Open	Open	Open
		from 12th	Open	Open	Open	Open
			Open	Open	Open	Open
			Open	Open	Open	Open
			Open	Open	Open	Open
			Open	Open	Open	Open
			Open	Open	Open	Open
			Open	Open	Open	Open
Open	Open		Open	Open	Open	Open
			Open	Open	Open	Open
			Open	Open	Open	Open
			Open	Open	Open	Open
			Open	Open	Open	Open
			Open	Open	Open	Open
			Open	Open	Open	Open
	Open	Open	Open	until 20th		
				from 21st	Open	Open
	Open	Open	Open	until 20th		
				from 21st	Open	Open
	Open	Open	Open	until 20th		
				from 21st	Open	Open
Open	Open	Open	Open	until 20th		
				from 21st	Open	Open
Open	Open	Open	Open			

Open and closed seasons in Northern Ireland

TRUE GAME	JAN	FEB	MAR	APR	MAY
Common pheasant					
Red-legged partridge					
Grey partridge					
Red grouse					
Brown hare					
WILDFOWL					
Woodcock					
Snipe					
Mallard					
Teal					
Wigeon					
Canada goose					
Greylag					
Pink-footed goose					
Golden plover					
Coot and moorhen					
DEER					
Red deer, male					
Red deer, female					
Fallow deer, male					
Fallow deer, female					
Sika deer, male					
Sika deer, female					
Muntjac deer, both sexes					

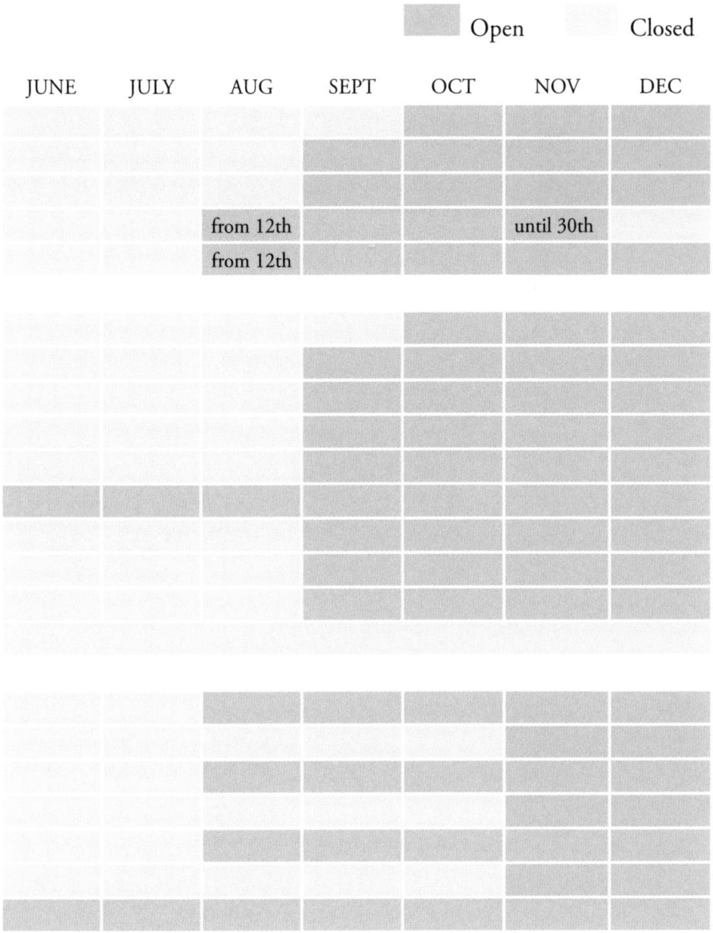

Open　　　Closed

JUNE	JULY	AUG	SEPT	OCT	NOV	DEC

from 12th — until 30th

from 12th

Game Species

True game species

This is the group of animals listed in the Game Act 1831 and in terms of flavour it contains some real heavyweights, such as grouse and hare. It is important to note that some of the species covered here have now become quite rare and, although still legally fair game, their pursuit has become rightly controversial. Some landowners and gamekeepers make active conservation of such species a priority – even as they choose to bag a few specimens a year 'for the pot'. However, several of the true game species exist in abundance, owing to good habitat management, as well as rearing and release systems such as those used for pheasants (see p.20).

Comparative size of true game species (male)

Ptarmigan

Grey partridge

Red-legged partridge

Red grouse

Black grouse

Mountain hare

Brown hare

Common pheasant

| 0 | 20 | 40 | 60 | 80 |

Centimetres

A pair of cock pheasants foraging for food

Common pheasant *Phasianus colchicus*

NOMENCLATURE	Hen (*f*); cock (*m*); poult (*young*); brace (*pair*); brood (*family group*); flock (*group*)
CONSERVATION STATUS	Abundant population, often supported by release birds
HABITAT	Pretty much anywhere rural, especially woodland, farmland, moorland and marshland
HUNTING SEASON	1 Oct–1 Feb (England, Wales and Scotland); 1 Oct–31 Jan (N Ireland)

I feel impertinent calling the pheasant 'common': it's an aristocratic bird, which struts about the countryside as if it owns the place. It wanders the lanes, refusing to get out of the way of cars until it absolutely has to. This fantastically plumaged creature has a habit of looking at you in a disparaging manner as you walk towards it, with an expression that seems to say, '*Must* you exist near me?'

Nevertheless, common they are. The breeding population of wild pheasants is estimated at around 2 million, though every year something like 40 million birds are reared and released. In Devon, where I live, barely a day goes by when I don't see a cock bird parading around the fields in its glorious plumage. We have all become so familiar with the sight of these birds that it's hard to believe they are, in reality, interlopers originating from the exotic climes of Asia.

Although there are wild populations of pheasant in numerous locations across the UK, most of the birds you see have been released for shooting after being raised on game farms. Pheasant shooting is big business and the birds are killed in large numbers (see p.20). Unfortunately, however, pheasant meat is still not much in demand so, at the time of writing, these birds, once dead, have very little value.

The greatest demand for pheasant is from Europe but emerging producers in Eastern Europe have cornered that market, making export from the UK almost profitless. We need to develop a domestic market for this meat, and fast. In the meantime, you can enjoy this healthy and abundant source of protein at very little cost. It's often available for the asking.

In the kitchen

Most cooks are likely to encounter pheasant as their first whole game bird in the feather. That initial experience may be a little daunting but, once you've dealt with the gory bits, you will have a sizeable bird with a good flavour. This works very well for many different dishes, and once you know how to pluck or skin and gut

A hen pheasant in maize cover

a pheasant, there will be no stopping you. For all other game birds, you simply scale the procedure up or down based on their size.

As with geese, ducks and so many other game birds, you can't do with an old pheasant what you can with a younger one. Remember to look out for the horny feet and moth-eaten feathers that identify mature specimens (over 8 months old and in some cases much older). These creatures need careful handling to get the most out of them.

I recommend minimal hanging time for pheasant, as they taste best when very fresh (see p.140). If you want to roast the birds whole, then you're better off with a hen bird, since these are more tender (see Roasted hen pheasant, p.171). Don't even attempt to roast a pheasant whole after Christmas or a cock bird after the end of November, as they will have toughened up too much to be truly enjoyable, though pot-roasting can give you the upper hand if you're bent on serving the birds entire. If that's your intention, make sure you apply the 'break, twist and pull' method on the feet (see p.146) to remove as much of the tough sinew from the leg meat as possible.

When the season gets going and I find myself with a glut of pheasant, I always skin the birds without plucking them first, remove the meat and freeze it in packs for later use (sometimes after a quick cure or rub of marinade). This saves space and time, as well as ensuring that all the birds get used and none are wasted.

Although very tasty, pheasant meat is still relatively mild and delicate for game, which makes it extremely versatile. I like to use it to make Spicy fajitas (see p.195) or a Game curry (see p.240) for an ad hoc mid-week supper, or to bone out the thighs and barbecue them. The breasts also hot-smoke incredibly well (as for Quick-smoked duck, p.200) and make a delicious Game Caesar salad (see p.190).

Pheasant can be used in place of chicken in almost any recipe, adding a greater depth of flavour. Be warned, though: the drumstick of a pheasant is far removed from that of a chicken, being much tougher. I usually save the drumsticks up and make a batch of Game ragu (see p.175), so I can remove any sinew after cooking.

A brace of red-legged partridge

Red-legged partridge *Alectoris rufa*

NOMENCLATURE	Hen (*f*); cock (*m*); poult (*young*); brace (*pair*); brood (*family group*); covey (*group*)
CONSERVATION STATUS	Abundant population, mostly made up of released birds
HABITAT	Prefers moorland edges, downland and large open arable farms
HUNTING SEASON	1 Sept–1 Feb (England, Wales and Scotland); 1 Oct–31 Jan (N Ireland)

Grey partridge *Perdix perdix*

NOMENCLATURE	Hen (*f*); cock (*m*); poult (*young*); brace (*pair*); brood (*family group*); covey (*group*)
CONSERVATION STATUS	Population fluctuating or declining, though some stock raised and released for shooting
HABITAT	Lowland pastures and farmland
HUNTING SEASON	1 Sept–1 Feb (England, Wales and Scotland); 1 Oct–31 Jan (N Ireland)

The red-legged and grey partridge are very different creatures, but they share similarities of flavour and their stories are intertwined.

The red-legged partridge is native to Spain, France and Portugal and has a notable preference for sandy soil and warm weather. Red-legged partridges were introduced to the east of England around the end of the eighteenth century and, despite their preference for a dry climate, their population spread slowly across the country. These birds are often referred to as French partridges, or 'Frenchmen', not just because of their origins but also because their red legs were reminiscent of the French army's striking uniform.

Although most red-legged partridge you see will have been reared and released by gamekeepers, there is a strong wild breeding population. This is good news, as they are on the decline in their native lands. In comparison to pheasant, however, red-legged partridge is still quite a rare treat. Only around 8–10 million birds are released each year, compared to 40 million pheasants. (To put those numbers into perspective, around 850 million chickens are reared for meat in the UK each year.)

A grey partridge

The grey partridge, also known as the English partridge, is indigenous to our islands but you are far less likely to see one. Grey partridge were a beloved quarry of the gentlemen shooters of old, and the gamekeepers of the nineteenth century looked after them. By managing their natural predators, they were able to generate substantial numbers of wild birds for shooting.

But by the 1950s the mechanisation of agriculture and chemical management of crops led to a drastic decline in the grey partridge population. It became a much less reliable source of shooting, not to mention a serious conservation concern. Reared and released red-legged partridge – which have the useful habit of laying two clutches of eggs a year – were then introduced to fill the gap and still far outnumber the native grey partridge.

These days, grey partridge numbers are on the up, thanks to the careful study of their habitat and habits by the GWCT. This group has done impressive work to help reintroduce and better understand the wild grey partridge and, though there is still a long way to go, there are hopes that the numbers of this truly native bird can be revived. However, this can only happen with careful management. Grey partridge chicks rely heavily on an insect diet in their early lives and the parent birds need hedgerows and grassy field margins to successfully raise their young.

For now, though, you're unlikely to get the opportunity to cook and eat one. Although a few of these birds are reared and released for shooting, the killing of truly wild grey partridge is strictly controlled. It happens almost exclusively on a few carefully managed estates where the population is kept stable from year to year.

In the kitchen

The meat of the partridge is a delight. The grey is particularly flavoursome, but the red-legged is still very good. Lighter and sweeter than pheasant, the meat has a certain chicken-y quality. It is essential that partridge are dealt with as fresh as possible (i.e. not hung). A contributing factor to this is that the partridge season starts a month earlier than the pheasant season. The weather is often a lot milder, so they will deteriorate much more quickly between dispatch and chilling.

Their small size makes partridge a perfect main course portion. They are best plucked and dressed in the traditional manner because the meat tastes far better when cooked on the bone. Season the birds, rub with a little oil and sear in a hot ovenproof pan on their backs over a high heat until golden brown, then repeat on each leg and side. Once nicely browned all round, flip them on to their breasts for a couple of minutes, then return to their backs and roast in a hot oven (at 220°C/ Gas mark 7) for around 8 minutes. Rest for 10 minutes before serving.

Partridge breasts are lovely pan-fried, and if you have a lot of partridge to deal with, de-breasting them is quick and clean. The meat also lends itself well to a Game Caesar salad (see p.190) and Partridge with pumpkin and cider (see p.180).

Red grouse *Lagopus lagopus scotica*

NOMENCLATURE	Hen (*f*); cock (*m*); poult (*young*); brace (*pair*); covey (*group*); pack (*large group*)
CONSERVATION STATUS	Abundant population
HABITAT	Moorland
HUNTING SEASON	12 Aug–10 Dec (England, Wales and Scotland); 12 Aug–30 Nov (N Ireland)

Red grouse is the first game bird to become available each year. The opening day of the grouse season in August is referred to as the 'Glorious Twelfth' because it heralds the coming winter of game shooting.

The red grouse is a charmer. If you've ever seen one then you'll surely agree that with their slightly otherworldly appearance, these creatures are simply magical. They are considered the finest of sporting birds and most hunters hanker to one day shoot grouse – although that dream may be out of reach for all but the most lucky or well-off.

Red grouse are medium-sized and fast flying, achieving 130kph (80mph) even without wind to assist them. They hug the contours of the moor and use the wind to accelerate to breakneck speed. This skill stems from their need to avoid their main predators: birds of prey. Raptors love to eat grouse but, by flying close to the ground at high speed, the grouse make it very risky for birds of prey such as falcons to tackle them, as the falcons themselves risk serious injury from high-speed impact with the ground.

On the ground, red grouse are well camouflaged and their plumage is thick enough to shield them from the elements. It extends all the way down the feet to the claws, giving them a comical, sock-wearing look.

Red grouse are often referred to as wild birds, but I think this term needs some analysis. The 'natural' habitat of the red grouse is actually one of the most carefully managed environments you could think of. In order to ensure the survival of the maximum number of birds each year, ground predators and pests are controlled. Heather is also burned on a cyclical basis to rejuvenate the plants and provide the greatest amount of cover for the birds, as well as optimum conditions for nesting and feeding.

In addition, the birds are given preventative treatment for worms and other illnesses, via medicated grit put down on the moor, to make sure that as many as possible make it to adulthood. As any poultry farmer will tell you, a high worm count on the ground, plus unprotected birds, equals disaster. In the past, it was

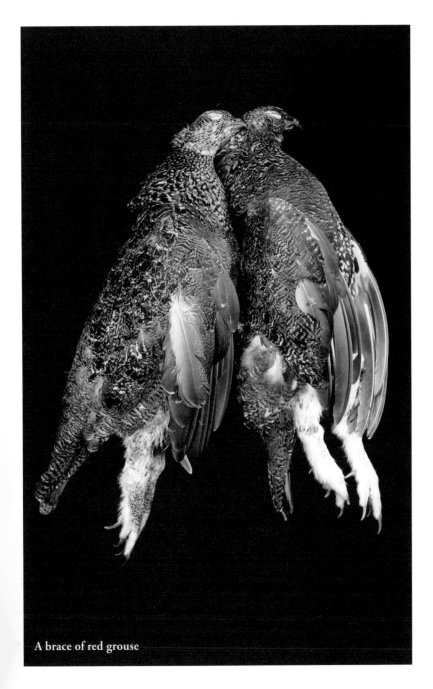

A brace of red grouse

A red grouse

accepted that worms would cause the grouse numbers on any given moor to 'crash' every few years and, as a result, hunting pressure in those years had to be carefully reduced to ensure that enough breeding pairs were left to produce chicks.

So while grouse are 'wild' in the sense that they are not reared and released, it's also fair to say that their abundance is somewhat artificial. However, land managed for grouse does benefit many other wild species such as the curlew, golden plover, black grouse and dunlin. Grouse moors are a great example of how habitat management can benefit many coexisting species, not just one.

In the kitchen

Red grouse has a formidable reputation as shooting quarry, which goes some way to explaining its desirability among those in the know. But I doubt it would have attained that status without also being one of the tastiest birds you're ever likely to encounter. Grouse meat is a joy. Its flavour is divine: strong enough to carry spices but sweet enough to serve simply, hot or cold, with little in the way of garnishes.

Old grouse (more than a season old) do need careful handling and will be both stronger in flavour and less tender. Ageing grouse can be difficult until you get the knack for it, but running a fingernail down the middle claw usually gives a reliable indication: if the joints are protruding, it's an older bird. Another giveaway is the claws themselves: young grouse, taken at the beginning of the season, will have soft, pliable nails the colour of light grey slate. As the season progresses, these will harden and darken.

It's also worth looking at the beak and general size and condition of the bird. A 'hard-shot' bird (one which has taken the full brunt of the shot) must be carefully inspected before cooking – you don't really want to hang these birds if you can help it; their sweetness lessens by the day.

Grouse pairs up well with strong flavours in stews and Game curry (see p.240). I also like to roast grouse whole with plenty of butter, using a very high heat for a short period of time, then let them rest for a good long while. Season the birds, rub with a little butter and sear in a hot ovenproof pan on their backs over a high heat until golden brown, then repeat on each leg and side. Once nicely browned all round, flip the birds on to their breasts for a couple of minutes, then return to their backs and roast in a hot oven (at 220°C/Gas mark 7) for around 12 minutes. Rest for 12 minutes before serving.

With an older bird, I remove the breasts, cure them briefly before cooking, and then serve them with noodles in a spicy broth made from the carcasses (see Old grouse noodle soup, p.182). Grouse bones make a strong but excellent stock that lends itself to Asian flavours, as well as more traditional soups or risotto. If you find yourself in the happy position of being inundated with fresh grouse, you can simply take the breast and leg meat off, without plucking (see pp.150–1).

A female black grouse (grey hen)

Black grouse *Tetrao tetrix*

NOMENCLATURE	Grey hen (*f*); cock (*m*); chick (*young*); brace (*pair*); covey (*group*); pack (*large group*)
CONSERVATION STATUS	Species under threat
HABITAT	Moorland
HUNTING SEASON	20 Aug–10 Dec (England, Wales and Scotland, except New Forest, Somerset and Devon, where it starts 1 Sept)

The black grouse, also known as the blackgame or grey hen, is the largest member of the grouse family in the country. This is a bird that you are highly unlikely ever to eat, as its numbers are in decline, and recent efforts to reintroduce it to various parts of the UK have had limited success.

Black grouse are very rare outside Scotland, although there are a few on Exmoor and in the Peak District and the Royal Society for the Protection of Birds (RSPB) is working very hard to increase populations on their reserves. Moorland owners and gamekeepers are also playing a significant role in the revival of the species and there are now around 5,500 breeding (lekking) males. It's good to see the numbers building again, but clearly this is nothing like enough to justify shooting them.

I include them here simply because they are named in the Game Act 1831, as are ptarmigan (see p.63), and to this day, there is still technically an open season for them. They are hunted in Europe, where numbers are more robust.

A ptarmigan in its winter plumage

Ptarmigan *Lagopus muta*

NOMENCLATURE	Hen (*f*); cock (*m*); chick (*young*); brace (*pair*); covey (*group*); pack (*large group*)
CONSERVATION STATUS	Population fluctuating or declining
HABITAT	High moorland and mountains
HUNTING SEASON	12 Aug–10 Dec (Scotland only)

A relic from the ice age, the ptarmigan is an impressive survivor. Only seen in the UK in the remote Highlands of Scotland, these birds are related to the far more common red grouse.

Another name for the ptarmigan is the croaker, due to the distinctive croaking call of the males. This fascinating bird changes its plumage in winter to blend into the snow, and then again in spring, returning to its summer coat of mottled grey and brown. The males have red wattles on their eyelids, which they can hide when they wish to conceal themselves.

These birds are rare: there are between 3,000 and 6,000 pairs in the UK and even the higher estimate is low enough to cause conservationists concern. I have never eaten one and do not expect to; I suspect you never will either, although a few ptarmigan are shot each year on specially arranged hunting trips. These are always limited to a brace of birds per hunter with the main part of the day being spent climbing the mountain to get to where the ptarmigan are gathered together in groups. They are, I am told, reluctant to fly, making them little of a challenge for the hunters.

It is interesting to note that in recent years the majority of these 'ptarmigan hunting trips' have been carried out by hunters with cameras rather than guns, with some shooters believing they are best left alone. There is no cause for concern over the tiny numbers that are shot each year, though I suspect these are mostly taken as trophies, a pursuit I find hard to understand.

A mountain hare growing into its summer coat

Mountain hare *Lepus timidus*

NOMENCLATURE	Doe (*f*); buck (*m*); leveret (*young*); down (*group*)
CONSERVATION STATUS	Migratory or fluctuating population
HABITAT	Mountains and high moorland
HUNTING SEASON	1 Aug–28 or 29 Feb (Scotland); no open season in England, Wales or N Ireland

Brown hare *Lepus europaeus*

NOMENCLATURE	Doe (*f*); buck (*m*); leveret (*young*); down (*group*)
CONSERVATION STATUS	Population fluctuating or declining
HABITAT	Lowland meadows and downlands
HUNTING SEASON	1 Oct–31 Jan (Scotland); 12 Aug–31 Jan (N Ireland); generally no closed season (England and Wales); see below for more details

Hare are fascinating creatures, steeped in myth and folklore – partly, perhaps, because of their shy and elusive nature. They have come to symbolise spring and fertility, as well as magic and mystery.

Only the mountain hare is indigenous to the UK. Because of its geographical spread, and its ability to change colour with the seasons to protect itself from predators, it has many names, including the blue hare, Alpine hare and snow hare. The larger brown hare was brought to the UK by the Romans, as part of their living larder.

Hunting these animals is difficult in the extreme. They nest in small indentations in the ground, known as 'makes', and the sight of a hare breaking cover and flying across a field is nothing short of awe-inspiring. They are the fastest land mammal in the UK, capable of running at around 56kph (35mph) and changing direction without slowing down.

A friend of mine who has tried shooting them in the snow in Scotland – where they are driven towards the guns by gamekeepers on quad bikes – likened it to attempting to shoot a snowflake with a blindfold on. Personally, I think that hare (and certainly fully grown brown hare) should be tackled with a small-bore rifle, since with a shotgun the chances of wounding, as opposed to a clean kill, are quite high for all but the most skilled of shots.

An adult brown hare

Hare hunting regulations are not straightforward either. If hare are on moorland or unenclosed land then there is a different rule applied under the Ground Game Act 1880 and its amendment in 1906. In these cases hare may only be taken with a firearm between 1st September and 31st March but may be taken by other means at different times. It's all quite complicated and I recommend you double-check your facts before undertaking any hare shooting.

The brown hare was once abundant, but suffered badly from loss of habitat during the agricultural 'revolution' of the 1960s and '70s. For many years, most shoots left them off the game card as there were so few of them around, but I'm glad to say they are now widespread, if not always abundant, once again. We do still need to be careful about hare populations. Many people feel the hare requires better legal protection. The problem is that giving it a specific closed season would be very difficult as it happily breeds most of the year round. An alternative approach, which some estates are now advocating, is to agree numbers for an annual cull based on records and breeding success.

In the kitchen

We can enjoy eating a few hare with a clear conscience – and eat them we should, for the meat is seriously good. I think it is best eaten very fresh so I recommend minimal hanging time (see p.140). Unlike rabbits, hares are hung with the guts in, which encourages the flavour to 'develop' quite rapidly. Skinning a hare is done in exactly the same way as for a rabbit (see pp.154–7), but it can be a bit more difficult, given that it's larger. You will need to gut the hare first (otherwise the stresses of skinning may cause an unpleasant and messy explosion) and you may well be surprised at the generous amount of meat on the carcass.

When you are cooking hare, it's important to treat it with reverence. It's a real culinary treat so take great care not to overcook it or dry it out, and partner it with sweet and delicate spices. One of my all-time favourite treats is hare shoulder cooked slowly under butter (see Potted hare, p.235). The saddle is also excellent roasted (see Roast saddle of hare with bay and sumac, p.233) or hot-smoked (as for rabbit, see Hot-smoked rabbit saddle, p.243).

Many chefs are, in my opinion, obsessed with 'jugging' hare – thickening the stewing juices with its blood. Frankly, if you want to use the blood, I think it's much better made into a Hare blood cake (see p.231), albeit a small one, which goes very well on toast.

Vermin

It seems unfair to call this resourceful, intelligent and seriously tasty group of animals 'vermin'. The term brings to mind unpleasant images: the idea of a mouse in the pantry or flies in the kitchen. But the meat of these creatures is some of the best around and to overlook them on your journey into wild meat would be foolhardy in the extreme. So try not to let the V-word put you off. It's a purely subjective term, applied to any creature with which we humans find ourselves in conflict (just as we call unwanted plants 'weeds', even though many of them are tasty and useful).

Vermin are the group of animals and birds hunted under what is termed the 'general licence'. That means that DEFRA has issued a licence to kill these pests in order to protect crops, or as a matter of public safety. That's not necessarily a green light to shoot them willy nilly. For example, if you wish to shoot pigeons to protect your crop (or with the consent of a landowner) you should be able to prove that you have tried frightening them away first, and that this has not worked. In short, other methods of control must be attempted before shooting can take place.

Wild boar
(not to scale)

Comparative size of vermin species

Wood pigeon

Rook

Grey squirrel

Rabbit

0   20   40   60

Centimetres

A pair of rooks in flight

Rook *Corvus frugilegus*

NOMENCLATURE	Rook (*f/m*); brancher (*young*); parliament or building (*group*)
CONSERVATION STATUS	Abundant population
HABITAT	Lowland farmland and woods
HUNTING SEASON	No closed season

Rooks are very common birds, but we never really seem to notice them until the early spring when they suddenly seem to be everywhere, making a racket, squabbling, courting and trying to build a nest with materials mostly stolen from another nest. They are remarkably social birds and belong to the crow family (more properly known as corvids).

Rooks can be tricky to distinguish from other black crow-like birds and this is made harder because they often congregate with jackdaws. Tasty though jackdaw can be, it is rooks that I'm after whenever I grab my shotgun in the early summer. Rooks have large, pale, ferocious-looking beaks and stunning black feathers with a purplish iridescence; mature rooks have pale patches on their faces around the beak. Jackdaws are somewhat smaller and have white-rimmed eyes and grey hoods.

You will definitely see rooks out and about in both small and large groups, foraging for food together; their Latin name, *Frugilegus,* literally means 'food gatherers'. If you live rurally, locating a nearby rookery will be easy – just follow the noise and commotion in early spring and you will find yourself a whole parliament of rooks.

Rooks eat some farm pests, such as daddy longlegs larvae or 'leatherbacks' but the trouble is they often get at them by the expedient of simply pulling up freshly sprouted cereal crops. Sadly, clever and tool-using as they are, rooks have yet to learn to replant the seedlings. This, coupled with their penchant for the odd cropful of grain and the occasional tendency to eat songbird eggs, has earned them a place on the general licence and they are fair game all year round.

I would strongly encourage you to try rook, if you haven't already. It's a seriously tasty bird and the abundance of this charming corvid is clear for all to see. Rooks are often shot in reasonable numbers and so should be relatively easy to come by. If you know a local farmer or gamekeeper, they will know where to lay their hands on some.

The young, just-about-to-fledge birds are known as 'branchers', and if you're out to bag one in the traditional way by climbing the tree and helping yourself, be warned – it's not as easy as it looks and the birds can lead you on a merry dance

A rook displaying the pale skin around its bill

from branch to branch, making them exceedingly difficult to grasp. It is madness to attempt without the proper safety equipment.

In the kitchen

Young brancher rooks are the nicest to eat, and the flavour of their meat rivals even that of pigeon. Hanging rook is entirely unnecessary except for the older birds and even then a day or two will be plenty (see p.140). The meat from older birds can be put through the sausage machine or used for a game pie.

Don't overcook rook, as it is best served medium-rare. I often pluck and gut a few branchers before roasting them whole. Season the birds, rub with a little oil and sear in a hot ovenproof pan on their backs over a high heat until golden brown, then repeat on each leg and side. Once nicely browned all round, flip them on to their breasts for a couple of minutes, then return to their backs and roast in a hot oven (at 220°C/Gas mark 7) for around 5 minutes. Allow to rest for 5 minutes before serving.

However, as the black feathers are time-consuming and fiddly to remove, I soon tire of plucking these birds for roasting and move on to simply removing the breasts and cooking them in a frying pan. I then slice them to add to salads, my favourite being a Game Caesar salad (see p.190) with rook in place of the more common chicken.

A pair of wood pigeons in a rural habitat

Wood pigeon *Columba palumbus*

NOMENCLATURE	Pigeon (*f/m*); squab (*young*); flock or dropping (*group*)
CONSERVATION STATUS	Abundant population
HABITAT	Commonly woods and farmland, but more or less anywhere except mountains and moorland
HUNTING SEASON	No closed season

Could there be a more perfect wild bird than the common wood pigeon? For me, the meat from this humble creature represents one of the greatest culinary delights out there. It tastes indulgently rich, even though there is sometimes an absence of fat. The layers of flavour are countless, even changing with the seasons owing to the bird's diet and age – younger birds are a little sweeter and milder.

I once had a job de-breasting pigeons. I stood in a concrete shed for hours on end, alone with a sharp knife, a radio and seemingly endless feed sacks stuffed with dead birds. As jobs go, it was pretty monotonous, but even handling literally thousands of dead pigeons every week failed to spoil the effect that the meat had on my palate. Needless to say, I became fairly proficient at de-breasting pigeons (in fact I could actually do it with my eyes shut), and almost as good at sneaking the odd half-dozen plump breasts into my lunch box for illicit consumption back at home.

I'm sure everyone who lives in the UK is familiar with what a pigeon looks like, but we need to be clear on the difference between wood and feral pigeons. The wood pigeon, as the name suggests, is a bird of the woods. Though wood pigeons often flock together in large numbers when threatened, they are more typically seen in groups of two to eight. The feral pigeon (*Columba livia*), commonly seen congregating in towns and cities in huge gangs awaiting the next meal, is a descendant of the rock pigeon that once served as a postal service. I've never, to my knowledge, eaten a feral pigeon and I'm not planning to change that any time soon.

Wood pigeons are, without doubt, one of the great agricultural pests. They have the ability to hatch brood after brood of chicks pretty much all year round, particularly if the weather remains mild throughout the winter. It's not at all uncommon to see hundreds of birds feeding on a single cereal or vegetable field. Naturally, the farmers who have planted these crops are reluctant to allow the ever-hungry wood pigeon to devour them. Pigeons are savvy and soon learn the difference between a bird-scaring gas gun and a real threat, so the effectiveness of the former is limited. That's where shooting comes in.

Incidentally, shooting a wood pigeon in flight is one of the hardest things to do within the sphere of hunting; a good pigeon shot must be a highly skilled marksman and their services are in great demand.

In the kitchen

Plucking pigeons is a messy business, as the feathers are fluffy and tend to end up everywhere. But with younger birds it's worth the effort because you can then roast them whole. Season the birds, rub them with a little pork fat or butter and sear in a hot ovenproof pan on their backs over a high heat until golden brown, then repeat on each leg and side. Once nicely browned all round, flip them on to their breasts for a couple of minutes, then return to their backs and roast in a hot oven (at 220°C/Gas mark 7) for around 5 minutes. Rest for 10 minutes before serving; they should be pink, but not bloody.

With older, larger birds, I would recommend removing and eating only the breasts and not bothering to pluck the whole thing. A favourite recipe of mine is Pigeon with blackberries and chanterelles (see p.187).

I love cooking pigeon breasts in all sorts of ways. They work brilliantly on the barbecue and I think they are better than beef when your inner carnivore demands steak and chips. But they are also delicious given a quick hot-smoking (as for Quick-smoked duck, see p.200) or even delicately cured. Pigeon and bacon burgers (see p.189) are particularly special and a Game curry (see p.240) made with pigeon is out of this world. I could go on for hours about the meat of these fascinating birds, but the one thing you really need to know is this: either cook them medium-rare or long and slow. An overcooked pigeon breast is like school-dinner liver... and you don't want that.

Rabbit *Oryctolagus cuniculus*

NOMENCLATURE	Doe (*f*); buck (*m*); kitten (*young*); bury or down (*group*)
CONSERVATION STATUS	Abundant population
HABITAT	Pretty much anywhere rural and suburban including farmland, parks, heathland, moorland and the seaside
HUNTING SEASON	Generally no closed season anywhere in the UK; see below for more details

There can be no better example of a more mixed-up approach to animals than our relationship with the rabbit. We eat it (though not nearly enough), we make a pet of it, and we also make a pest of it. Confusing, isn't it?

Why people are so fond of keeping rabbits as pets is clear: they are very easy to care for, and they cost little to feed. They also have a friendly look about them, with their furry faces and large eyes – characteristics that humans are programmed to respond positively to, and this puts many people off eating them (though, oddly enough, most children seem happy to tuck in).

It's hard to imagine a time without rabbits in the UK, but they are an introduced species – by the Romans again. Common (or European) rabbits were once farmed in warrens for their meat and fur, but inevitably some of them escaped and established substantial wild populations. As the trend for eating rabbit and wearing their skins dwindled, so their numbers spiralled out of control.

Rabbits, along with pigeons, are the arch-enemy of the modern cereal farmer, or, indeed, grass-growing dairy or sheep farmer. The reasons are obvious. One rabbit can, and will, eat around half a kilo of grass (or young barley, wheat, or seedlings) a day. This comes to 182.5kg a year for each rabbit, or 1.825 tonnes for ten rabbits – about an acre's worth of grass. Ten rabbits can very quickly become a hundred, and so the population must be controlled if they are not to devastate our crops. They are the best example of what I like to call 'accidentally farmed meat' – an incidental by-product of agriculture.

In 1950 there was an attempt to control the number of wild rabbits in Australia, involving the deliberate spread of myxomatosis, a disease that can have devastating effects on rabbit colonies. It's as inhumane a way of culling a group of animals as you can imagine and the deliberate introduction of the disease was never sanctioned by the British government as it had been in Australia. However, incidences of myxomatosis began to occur here a few years later – perhaps the result of desperate

farmers releasing infected rabbits. By 1955, an estimated 90% of our rabbit population had been wiped out. Nevertheless, the rabbits recovered and most colonies developed an immunity. Although its impact is far less than before, myxomatosis is still about. An infected rabbit is easy to spot because of its swollen, inflamed eyes. When still alive, it will also behave oddly, not reacting to danger.

What this disease has done exceedingly well is to put many people off the idea of eating rabbit meat, which is a shame. It is very easy to identify, both in a living and a dead rabbit, and the chances of an infected animal getting into the food chain are incredibly small. No hunter or butcher worth their salt would allow it. You wouldn't want to eat a myxi rabbit – it may well be in very poor condition and infected with other things, such as pasteurella, due to its compromised immune system – but humans cannot contract the disease.

Although you are free to hunt rabbits all year round, you need to be aware that there are certain restrictions on moorland and unenclosed land. In England and Wales, rabbits may be killed in these habitats from 1st September to 31st March, but only with firearms between 11th December and 31st March. In Scotland they may be killed all year round on these terrains but only with firearms between 1st July and 31st March.

In the kitchen

Rabbit should be eaten fairly fresh and only hung for a very short period – as little as a couple of days will be more than enough for all but the oldest and toughest of specimens (see p.140). If you don't know how to skin a rabbit (see pp.154–7), your butcher should be able to supply you with one already prepared. Just make sure you ask for wild rabbit, or you could end up with an imported farmed one, which won't have the same flavour; there are also serious welfare concerns about farmed rabbit.

Rabbit makes some of the tastiest meals out there, and it is very low in fat. The younger ones are quite tender enough to be roasted in a hot oven and then simply chopped up to serve. Season the rabbit and place in a hot roasting tray. Scatter over a few bay leaves, plus a few bits of bacon or chorizo if you like. Roast at 220°C/ Gas mark 7 for 10 minutes, then turn over and roast for another 5 minutes before removing from the oven. Leave to rest for 15 minutes before serving.

Older rabbits (the best indicator of age is size) tend to be tougher and skinning them is more difficult. These more mature specimens are better braised, or cooked as a Game curry (see p.240), Game ragu (see p.175), potted (as for Potted hare, see p.235) or confit as Game rillettes (see p.215). The cheffy part of me loves to serve rabbit three or four different ways on the same plate, but it's a lot of effort. One thing I always recommend, though, is the liver – especially if you have a good batch of fresh young bunnies. It makes a quick and excellent pâté: Tuscan rabbit livers (see p.238), which is delicious spread on toast.

Grey squirrel *Sciurus carolinensis*

NOMENCLATURE	Sow (*f*); boar (*m*); kit or pup (*young*); pest or drey (*group*)
CONSERVATION STATUS	Abundant population
HABITAT	Woodland and suburban gardens and parks
HUNTING SEASON	No closed season

Squirrel is a great creator of temporary vegetarians at supper tables, so much so that I often fib and tell people that we are eating rabbit, which has a similar flavour. The most creative stage name for squirrel I've come across is 'flightless partridge'. Why some people have issues eating squirrel while they will happily eat other meats is beyond me. Perhaps these charismatic garden inhabitants are perceived to be more in the pet camp than the things-to-eat camp, but that's a shame – to me, they represent fresh, tasty and free-range meat there for the taking.

This interloper to our lands is one for which we must squarely take the blame ourselves (it wasn't, for once, the Romans who brought them over). The first pair of grey squirrels was released in Cheshire in 1876 as a quirky garden attraction, and they soon became a fashion item for those wanting to 'keep up with the Joneses'. Before you could say Jack Robinson, grey squirrels had taken over the world – as far as the native red squirrel was concerned, anyway.

Grey squirrels compete with the native red squirrel for food and territory and, as they are larger and more aggressive, the more diminutive red has vanished from all but the most remote parts of the UK. The grey squirrel is also able to digest a wider variety of foods, enabling it to survive in greater numbers – the UK population currently stands at around 2.5 million, though I suspect the true figure is higher. And as if that wasn't enough, grey squirrels can carry squirrelpox, which although harmless to them, is deadly for red squirrels.

Grey squirrels are good at overcoming challenges and will happily take food from bird tables as well as anywhere else within a short range of their dreys (nests). They come into conflict with foresters, because they damage young trees, and with gamekeepers, because they eat feed intended for game birds, which explains their 'vermin' status.

Squirrels are often poisoned by pest-control specialists, so any would-be squirrel hunters should be wary: ask a lot of questions of the landowner when acquiring permission to bag a few for your lunch. Anyone selling squirrel meat has a legal responsibility to ensure that it is safe to eat, so I would recommend buying from a reputable game dealer.

In the kitchen

Squirrel meat makes for an unusual and tasty treat. Preparing one for cooking is straightforward: just imagine it's a very small rabbit with a long tail, cut off the tail and you won't go wrong (see the rabbit preparation guide on pp.154–7).

Young or 'new season' squirrels, shot in early autumn when they start to fatten themselves up for winter, are the best to eat. Light in flavour, a lot like rabbit and ever so tender, they cook quickly on the barbecue or in the oven. Roasted squirrels are delicious (see p.228), often with a nutty flavour, which is perhaps unsurprising.

Older squirrels, which will be larger in size and far harder to skin than younger specimens, should be given the low-and-slow treatment to bring out the best in them, and I often include some pork fat to help them along. Leave the squirrels whole or split the back legs and place in a large casserole. Add garlic, carrots, wine, herbs and enough stock to just cover. Put the lid on and cook slowly in a low oven (at 140°C/Gas mark 1) for at least 2 hours, until the meat is tender.

I also mince squirrel meat to make a Game ragu (see p.175). Note that you should never eat the brain of a squirrel, cooked or uncooked, as it carries prion proteins that could be passed on to the person eating them, possibly causing an illness a little like Mad Cow Disease. Cooking does not entirely destroy these proteins, so it's best to avoid consuming them altogether.

Wild boar *Sus scrofa*

NOMENCLATURE	Sow (*f*); boar (*m*); piglet (*young*); sounder or singular (*group*)
CONSERVATION STATUS	Fluctuating population
HABITAT	Woodland and farmland with woodland borders
HUNTING SEASON	No closed season

Although they are a native species, truly wild boar vanished in the UK until some more intrepid specimens found their way out from farms in the late 1980s. Since then their range and population has been the subject of much debate among hunting and farming groups, as well as conservation organisations. We know for certain that there are now naturalised, truly wild boar living in our woodlands, and a conservative estimate of their number is one million. Their populations are centred particularly around the Forest of Dean, but they can also be found across the Southeast and Southwest of England, as well as in an increasing number of other locations around the UK.

Wild boar are remarkably reclusive, which is quite good news given their size, although it's extremely unlikely that a wild boar would attack you unless you threatened the boar or its young. Boar mostly forage for food at night. Socially, the males tend to be loners, while the matriarchal sows hang out with sexually immature offspring in family groups known as 'sounders'. The young males will leave their group to find sows of their own once they reach sexual maturity.

It's a shame that wild boar are still considered a pest, but they are omnivorous creatures and do love nothing more than rooting about in the topsoil for tasty treats. That's where they come into conflict with farmers.

While boar numbers have to be managed in much the same way as deer, boar-hunting is currently completely unregulated. It's perfectly legal to shoot any boar, with any firearm. It's up to the hunter to choose not to kill animals with dependent young, and to use the correct firepower to do the job humanely. The vast majority of hunters will do so, drawing up a proper cull plan for the boar in the woodlands they manage the hunting on, and using the appropriate rifle with the correct ammunition to do the job properly and safely. But the lack of clarity on this issue leaves room for bad practice without recourse to the law. Wild boar have a place in our wild habitats and they deserve the respect of a closed season and proper control on hunting.

I once spent a memorable few hours up a tree in a hide with a cameraman and a wild boar hunter, in the dark, trying to film the hunter taking a boar. Sadly (for us, that is) the boar failed to put in an appearance. But I can confirm that

if you ever need to get to know a couple of people really quickly, then locking yourself in a wooden box with them, 10 metres up a tree, with one of you holding a high-velocity rifle and another filming everything that goes on, will surely get you results. We remain friends to this day.

Though you are unlikely to chance upon a boar while walking in the woods, you may well come across signs of them: wallows and tracks are a dead giveaway, as is well-rooted-up ground.

In the kitchen

Wild boar are porky in flavour, as you would expect, but the meat is dark, with a much fuller flavour than the meat from even the best slow-grown, free-range rare-breed pigs. Because of the coarse, hairy bristles that cover the entire boar, the carcass always needs to be skinned, meaning you don't get any crackling into the bargain – but the meat is so good, you won't miss it. A whole boar is best hung for a few days before skinning, to make the process easier. It can then be hung a little longer if required (see page 140).

Wild boar meat is revered and celebrated throughout Europe; the hams and salami are jealously guarded and saved for the most special of occasions. Although getting hold of wild boar meat can be tricky in the UK, if you persevere you will find a source.

A good local butcher should be able to get you some boar meat, though this may well come from a farmed animal rather than a truly wild one, and the flavour, though excellent, won't be quite the same as the real thing.

If somebody offers you a whole boar then make sure you know what you are getting yourself into: a large one can weigh in excess of 150kg. I was once offered a whole wild boar for the asking and was delighted to accept. But when it arrived, it was so huge I had to buy another freezer to fit all the meat in. It took me two whole days to process the meat. However, if you're prepared for the task, it is simple enough to complete. (Simply follow the instructions for skinning and butchering a deer on pp.158–167.)

If you are buying from a game dealer or local butcher, the skinning and jointing will have been done for you and all that's left for you to decide is how to cook it. I love a wild boar steak cooked in a cast-iron pan in the wood oven, but it's just as good char-grilled or barbecued like any other steak. Be careful not to overcook it, but you don't want it rare either. It is best medium cooked: allow 4 minutes each side for a 1.2cm (½ inch) thick steak.

Pan-fried breaded escalopes (see p.226) are also a quick and convenient way to cook the seamed-out haunch or loin. Wild boar is also excellent in a Game curry (see p.240) or Spicy fajitas (see p.195), or minced for a Game ragu (see p.175) to serve with your favourite pasta.

Wildfowl

Wildfowl is the term used to describe wild birds that are especially shot for eating. There are around 20 different species that can be shot in the UK, depending on where you are in the country. I've listed in detail the most commonly taken species, with a mention for the others as I go along.

The life cycle of wildfowl follows the ebb and flow of nature. Many wildfowl will overwinter here in the UK before returning north, east and west to their native breeding territories – mating, laying eggs and rearing young to coincide with an abundant food source on which to feed them, and in time for the young to reach maturity before the long migration to warmer wintering grounds. Some wildfowl also spend their whole lives in the UK without ever migrating, and these we rather charmingly refer to as residents.

Hunting wildfowl is serious business and the rewards are well worth the effort but I would strongly advise careful research before attempting it. Of course, you will need permission, a shotgun certificate and the right kind of shot. The main problem, though, is that wildfowl species are not only tricky to identify in many cases, but are often best shot in the near darkness of dawn and dusk. Accidentally kill a protected species and you will find yourself in very hot water.

That said, wildfowl do offer some of the finest meat that you can find, and I suspect that this is the reason why a hard core of expert wildfowling hunters exists. Out there come rain, wind or snow, up to their chins in mud, they are happy to risk their necks on estuary flats for the chance to bag just a few of these birds.

Wildfowl fall into four basic categories: waders, such as snipe and woodcock; ducks, such as mallard, teal and wigeon; geese, including Canada, greylag and pink-footed; and others, such as coot and moorhen. I won't be exploring this last category as, frankly, I have never met anyone who had a good word to say about eating a moorhen.

The moorhen is, in fact, the butt of the oldest recipe joke in the world, which goes like this: One man asks another, 'Do you have a good way of cooking moorhens? They always turn out tough when I cook them.'

The other replies, 'Oh, you need to use the brick method. That's what I do and it improves them no end.'

'The brick method?' asks the first.

'Yeah, you pluck 'em and draw 'em and place them on a brick. Put the whole lot in the oven for an hour and then take it out. Throw away the moorhen and eat the brick. Much better!'

So, there you have it. I said it was an old joke.

Waders

The waders most often shot in the UK are the common snipe and the woodcock. The smaller jacksnipe is protected in England, Wales and Scotland but it is still sometimes shot in Ireland. The conservation status of the jacksnipe is an issue, and as a matter of course, I wouldn't choose to shoot one.

Then we have the golden plover. Many people don't shoot golden plover even if the opportunity arises, preferring to leave them alone. There are around 40,000 breeding pairs resident in Northwest England, Northern Ireland and Scotland, though their numbers swell to over 400,000 during the winter migration. I'm told golden plover are delicious, though I have never eaten one myself and, given their amber status on the RSPB's conservation list, I'm not planning to try one anytime soon. The threat to them from shooting is minimal, though I have yet to find any reliable figures on how many are shot each year in the UK.

Ducks

The depth of flavour in wild ducks that have lived a free life, eating anything from acorns and grass to wheat, barley, pondweed and small invertebrates, is simply magnificent. Treat the meat with the utmost respect, waste as little as possible and, if you're sharing your meal with others, make sure they bring good wine. I have been known to drive across two counties to visit friends who have had a successful duck flight, just to collect a couple of wild mallard or teal. They are that good.

There are nine species of wild duck shot in the UK: gadwall, goldeneye, mallard, pintail, pochard, shoveler, teal, tufted duck and wigeon. (In Northern Ireland, the scaup is also a target species.) The most frequently shot ducks are teal, mallard and wigeon.

Geese

There are four different types of goose shot in the UK: Canada, greylag, pink-footed and white-fronted. I have not included an entry for the latter as you are far less likely to encounter a white-fronted goose while hunting, except in certain locations (Hampshire, Scotland and Kent). However, it is not endangered or of a particular conservation concern, so if you are lucky enough to come by one, treat it as you would a pink-footed goose, which is similar in size.

As with ducks, the usual method of obtaining one is to shoot it with a shotgun at dawn or dusk, either during the geese's flight off the water to feed in the early hours, or on their way back to the water in the evening.

Geese fly significantly faster and higher than ducks, and as a rule, they are less predictable too, so it takes considerable skill to shoot them. It's a specialist form of hunting that only the most dedicated wildfowlers have any regular success with, making wild goose a rare ingredient in the kitchen.

Comparative size of wildfowl species

Snipe

Teal

Woodcock

Wigeon

Mallard

Pink-footed goose

Greylag

Canada goose

0   20   40   60   80

Centimetres

A woodcock camouflaged in its woodland habitat

Woodcock *Scalopax rusticola*

NOMENCLATURE	Woodcock (*f/m*); chick (*young*); brace (*pair*); fall (*group*)
CONSERVATION STATUS	Migratory or fluctuating population
HABITAT	Woodland; less commonly heathland and marshland
HUNTING SEASON	1 Oct–31 Jan (England, Wales, Scotland and N Ireland)

These wild creatures are among the finest-tasting animals on the planet, but you are unlikely to come by one for the pot unless you shoot it yourself – which is considered by hunters to be quite a challenge. In fact, the phrase 'a feather in your cap' comes from the tradition of tucking the pin feathers of your first woodcock into your hunting cap.

Woodcock are not particularly rare and, in the shooting season, their number increases due to the 'fall' or migration of birds coming from more northerly climes. But the difficulty of bagging them, coupled with their reputation as excellent table fare, means that any that are shot almost always go home with one of the hunters at the end of a shoot day and very few are ever for sale. A more reliable way of getting a couple for the pot would be to talk to someone who shoots a few and owes you a favour (or indeed about whom you have some useful secret up your sleeve, which they don't wish others to know).

Woodcock appear along the east coast of England in late autumn, most prolifically around the time of the November full moon. According to legend, the explanation for their sudden annual appearance is because they hatch from mermaids' purses on the beach.

These days, we know that they actually arrive exhausted after an epic migration, often having flown over 2,000 miles from their summer haunts in Scandinavia, the Baltic States and Russia. The birds are so drained that they simply stop on the beach to recover at least some strength before heading off to their preferred wintering wood. It is this habit that led people to the romantic misconception that they had been born from the sea.

Even now we are only just beginning to understand the migratory habits of these forest-dwelling enigmas and the more we learn, the more extraordinary they seem. The GWCT's pioneering 'Woodcock Watch' project, which is tracking the birds' migrations via satellite, is doing a great deal to throw light on the subject. Woodcock are mostly nocturnal, lying up in the woods all day, and using their

A brace of woodcock

perfect camouflage to avoid detection. At dusk, they fly out of the woods to nearby fields to feed on worms and other sub-surface treats, using their distinctive long, sensitive bills.

In days past, fine nets were set up on long poles to catch the birds on their evening flight paths, a practice known as 'night-netting'. The woodcock could not see these nets and would fly straight into them, getting trapped. They were then retrieved by the hunters and sent, alive, to market. This practice was used to trap many different wildfowl – a land-based equivalent of gathering fish from the ocean.

During the day, we see woodcock only when they are disturbed in the woods; they take flight with astonishing acceleration and are incredibly agile in the air. It is their sudden, unexpected appearance, diminutive size and jinking flight that make any marksman proud to have shot one. But these days, many don't even try. The general rule among those that do is, 'Don't shoot it unless you want to eat it and don't shoot more than a few each season.'

In the kitchen

When, and if, you are lucky enough to lay your hands on a woodcock, pluck it carefully but don't gut it. The birds only feed at night and empty their bowels upon taking flight, so the digestive tract will be empty and the guts safe for eating.

Roast the birds whole, hot and fast (see Roasted woodcock or snipe, p.185). There is also a tradition of eating the brain from the split roasted head of the bird and that too is tasty, though I don't often bother with this.

Snipe *Gallinago gallinago*

NOMENCLATURE	Snipe (*f/m*); chick (*young*); wisp (*group*)
CONSERVATION STATUS	Population fluctuating or declining
HABITAT	Water meadows, wetlands, heathland and moorland
HUNTING SEASON	12 Aug–31 Jan (England, Wales and Scotland); 1 Sept–31 Jan (N Ireland)

Ever wondered where the term 'sniper' comes from? It's all down to this little bird. Snipe are small, fast and erratic fliers. They gain altitude rapidly and take flight at the slightest hint of danger, often uttering a shrill call of rebuke. They are so difficult to shoot that in America, going on a 'snipe hunt' is a euphemism for having an almost impossible task or futile mission.

If you have ever surprised a small brown bird that then flitted away from you as you walked over marshy ground or water meadows in the winter, it's almost certain to have been a snipe. If it happens again, watch the bird's flight path closely. Snipe tend to head away from you, in large circles or zigzag patterns, and they get higher all the time until you lose sight of them. If you think you have seen a snipe but it drops back down into cover, it was probably the smaller jacksnipe (*Lymnocryptes minimus*).

Although snipe are relatively common in certain areas and the shooting of them is difficult in the extreme, we should take care to avoid overtaxing their numbers by shooting too many. The population is estimated to be around 80,000 breeding pairs – mostly in the far north of the UK – with an overwintering migration population in the south of around a million visiting birds during winter. This fluctuation and the fact that many snipe are migratory makes it difficult to ensure that only a sustainable harvest is taken. Conservation must be the priority.

In the kitchen

As with its larger cousin, the woodcock, you're unlikely to be able to get hold of snipe unless you know some keen hunters. And they're not likely to give them up cheaply, given the difficulty of acquiring them and the rewards they offer at the supper table. If you do manage to lay your hands on a 'finger of snipe' (the number, i.e. three, that you can hold between your fingers), you are in for a very special treat. Don't be put off by their small size; snipe meat is a delicacy that packs a flavour punch. Like woodcock, the birds are cooked guts and all. Straightforward roasting is the best way forward (see Roasted woodcock or snipe, p.185).

Mallard drakes with their breeding season plumage

Mallard *Anas platyrhynchos*

NOMENCLATURE	Hen or duck (*f*); drake (*m*); duckling (*young*); brace (*pair*); flock, paddling or sord (*group*)
CONSERVATION STATUS	Abundant population, often supported by release birds
HABITAT	Ponds, rivers, shoreline, estuaries and wetlands
HUNTING SEASON	1 Sept–31 Jan, extending to 20 Feb on the shoreline (England, Wales and Scotland); 1 Sept–31 Jan regardless of location (N Ireland)

This is your common or garden duck. The mallard is probably the first waterfowl any child learns to identify. It's very easy to tell the male from the female, because the drake has that eye-catching emerald green head with the white pastoral collar, while the female has mottled brown feathers. Outside the breeding season, the drakes' plumage becomes more like that of the females, but you can still identify them by the yellow colour of their bills and the greenish iridescence of their heads. The female has a fine orange and black bill.

In recent years there has been an upsurge in the number of reared mallard being released into the wild for shooting. This has led to an increase in the number of resident birds. The problem is that reared and released birds don't appear to be as good at breeding as their wild counterparts. In addition, the long-term trend for overwintering birds, many of which migrate here from Iceland and Northern Europe for the winter, is a slow decline, which may be down to climatic changes. The situation with released mallard will need monitoring to ensure that the wild population is protected for the future.

In the kitchen

The mallard is the largest of the dabbling ducks on the quarry list, and is about the same size as the rarer pintail (*Anas acuta*). Nonetheless, once it has been plucked and drawn, you may still be surprised at just how small it is compared to farmed ducks.

As more and more gamekeepers start to keep a couple of ponds for a duck drive, so the availability of wild mallard in farmers' markets and butchers' shops has increased. This has been nicely followed by a surge in demand and means you won't have too much trouble getting hold of some.

As with any wildfowl, mallard that have been shot 'hard' (taken the full brunt of the shot) should be used without delay and not hung. Use them as fresh as you

A mallard hen

can, and if you don't have time to pluck them, simply remove the legs and breasts. If you do not have the time for that, give them away to people who do.

Whether roasted or cooked in a more elaborate fashion, these birds are hard to beat. The duck flavour is underlain with a smooth richness that lends itself to all manner of different dishes. To roast them whole, season well and sear on their backs in a hot pan over a high heat until golden brown, then repeat on each leg and side. There is no need to add extra fat to the bird or the pan as there will be plenty released from the skin. Once nicely browned all round, flip them quickly on to the breasts for a couple of minutes, then return to their backs and roast in a hot oven (at 220°C/Gas mark 7) for around 15 minutes. Allow them to rest for a further 20 minutes before serving; they should be pink but not bloody.

A whole mallard that's been slow-roasted with aromatics is particularly good (see Slow-roast spiced soy duck, p.193). Mallard breasts are delicious pan-fried and served with redcurrant jelly or berries and mushrooms (see p.187). They also lend themselves beautifully to hot-smoking (see Quick-smoked duck, p.200). And they are great in stir-fries, Spicy fajitas (see p.195) and Game Caesar salad (see p.190). If you end up with more than a few mallard, Duck 'bacon' and eggs (see p.199) is the way to go; eating duck for breakfast in this way is one of my favourite winter treats. Older birds make a flavoursome soup (see Old grouse noodle soup, p.182).

All wild duck breasts, but mallard in particular, freeze successfully, as long as you exclude as much air as possible from the bag or wrapper. Defrosted, they work really well in stir-fries or fajitas (as above).

A cock teal, identified by its head plumage

Teal *Anas crecca*

NOMENCLATURE	Teal or duck (*f*); drake or cock (*m*); duckling (*young*); spring (*group*)
CONSERVATION STATUS	Migratory or fluctuating population
HABITAT	Ponds, shoreline, estuaries and wetlands
HUNTING SEASON	1 Sept–31 Jan, extending to 20 Feb on the shoreline (England, Wales and Scotland); 1 Sept–31 Jan regardless of location (N Ireland)

The common or Eurasian teal is held in high regard by hunters because of the shooting challenge it presents. As ever, it seems the tastier something is, the harder it is to get hold of. And teal really are tasty: one or two for the pot are a wonderful treat. They have a deep, rich flavour, not unlike that of goose.

Teal are small, dabbling ducks, meaning they feed head down in the water. They look a little like mallard, but are significantly smaller. They are usually shy of humans. A spring of teal taking to the air as you approach a quiet pond is quite a sight to behold – it's their swift ascent that has won them that collective noun. Around coastal areas you may well see a few goldeneye ducks (*Bucephala clangula*) alongside teal. These are around the same size but have very different markings, not to mention distinctive golden eyes.

Though there is a small breeding population in the UK, thought to be around 3,000 birds, most teal you see are overwintering here after a long migration flight from as far away as the Baltic and Siberia. The RSPB has expressed conservation concern over teal, but they are seldom shot in large numbers and the odd few taken for the larder are unlikely to make much of an impact on the population. As with all wild species, many conservation groups keep an eye on numbers, and spread the information via their membership and the media (see the Directory, p.248). Most hunters react swiftly to any decline by way of a self-imposed ban on shooting until the population is deemed to be within a safe margin.

In the kitchen

Unless it is badly damaged on one side, I always take the time to pluck and roast teal whole, as for mallard (see p.99), but allowing just 4 minutes in the oven and 5 minutes resting. I hardly ever adorn it beyond the salt and pepper treatment and I always serve it on its own, with a little fruit jelly. Redcurrant works well; crab apple is even better.

Wigeon *Anas penelope*

NOMENCLATURE	Hen or duck (*f*); drake (*m*); duckling (*young*); paddling or company (*group*)
CONSERVATION STATUS	Migratory or fluctuating population
HABITAT	Ponds, shoreline, estuaries and wetlands
HUNTING SEASON	1 Sept–31 Jan, extending to 20 Feb on the shoreline (England, Wales and Scotland); 1 Sept–31 Jan regardless of location (N Ireland)

This medium-sized duck is a little smaller than a mallard but larger than a teal. Confusingly, that makes it about the same size as a gadwall duck (*Anas strepera*) for which, in half-light, it can be mistaken. Its distinctive brown head is the wigeon's simplest identifying characteristic and explains its less common name – dun bird.

The number of wigeons in winter, particularly in coastal areas, can take your breath away, and it's not uncommon to see whole paddlings of them. But don't be fooled into thinking they are abundant. They group together in cold weather so you may be looking at every wigeon for miles around, all paddling in the same spot.

As with all ducks, wigeon were once netted on ponds in vast numbers, such was their abundance, but with the loss of many of their natural wetland habitats, notably in the Lincolnshire fens, we have fewer flocking here than in the past.

In the kitchen

People often say that you need to know what wigeon have been feeding on before you cook them, as they can have a very muddy flavour. I don't agree, although it's possible that birds from inland rivers may taste 'cleaner' than those that have spent a lot of time feeding in the mud on estuary flats. I suspect the real culprit here is too much hanging time. I would recommend a couple of days' hanging at most for any duck smaller than a mallard. I've always found the flavour from wigeon to be rich, deep and surprisingly sweet. There is something very satisfying about this and it feels very much like the right sort of thing to eat in the autumn and winter.

I think roasting is the best way with these little chaps. Very often I will simply remove the breasts for roasting. Sometimes, because wild ducks are far less fatty than farmed, I pluck the breasts before removing them so that I can leave the skin and fat in place. However, wigeon carry more fat at the beginning of the season, between early September and mid-November, making plucking more worthwhile.

Wigeon can be used in all recipes suitable for duck (see p.99). Should you manage to bag or, indeed, be given more than a few wigeon, the breasts freeze well.

Canada goose *Branta canadensis*

NOMENCLATURE	Goose (*f*); gander (*m*); gosling (*young*); gaggle, paddling or flock (*group*); skein (*group in flight*)
CONSERVATION STATUS	Abundant population
HABITAT	Lakes, rivers, wetlands, public parks and pretty much anywhere
HUNTING SEASON	No closed season

Despite being an introduced species, Canadas are the most common geese in the UK, seen everywhere from town parks to golf courses – wherever there is sufficient water and grazing. These birds are primarily herbivorous but will occasionally eat small fish and invertebrates.

Introduced to the country as part of King Charles II's waterfowl collection in St James' Park in 1665, they began interbreeding with other wild geese, creating all sorts of interesting hybrids. But by the 1960s, Canada geese numbers were mushrooming and causing a few problems. These geese are now often seen as pests. Beautiful as they are, they tend to make a bit of a mess with the amount of manure they leave behind them, not to mention the crops they can consume.

With around 62,000 breeding pairs and around 200,000 birds overwintering, you can begin to see the scale of the problem in some areas. Populations are monitored very carefully around the UK and Canada geese are culled in great numbers where they start to become a nuisance.

In the kitchen

Plucking and dressing any wild goose is a long, slow and tiresome process and after all that work, the rewards can be a little tough. Like all wild goose flesh, the meat tends to be very strong in flavour, ranging from rich to… well, frankly, pond water. If you are lucky enough to shoot a young goose, then it will be worth roasting, but it would need to be from that year's brood.

Assessing the age of these birds is important, to determine how you should cook them, but it can be tricky as there are many middle-aged geese around. Try bending the bill to see if it's flexible and see if you can tear the webbing on the feet. The older the bird the tougher the bill and webbing will be. If you're planning on roasting a young bird whole, hang it for a couple of days, pluck and dress it, then age it in the fridge for a few more days to improve the flavour and tenderness.

It is impractical to roast a goose by starting it off in a pan on the hob, as the size of the bird prohibits this. Bring the goose to room temperature before you start.

A pair of Canada geese in the reeds

Season the bird well, then place it on its back in a hot roasting tray in a hot oven at 220°C/Gas mark 7. Assuming the bird is around 3kg, give it 25 minutes, then turn it on to one side and give it another 10 minutes. Repeat on the other side and then turn the goose breast side down and give it 5 minutes. Now, turn off the oven but leave the bird inside for another 10 minutes before removing it. Allow it to rest for at least another 15 minutes before carving. Note that this time will give you perfectly cooked breast meat. You can remove the legs before resting the breast meat and return them to the oven to cook for longer.

Brining is a useful technique for goose. I occasionally remove the breasts from the carcass, tenderise them in a light brine, then roast them. They can be very good indeed if the bird is a young one. Make a simple cold water brine by mixing one part salt and one part sugar to ten parts water and adding some aromatics of your choice; bay and star anise are both very good. Place the goose breasts in the brine for an hour or two before removing them and allowing them to dry. Then cook as you would any other steak-like piece of meat.

If you can only lay your hands on a mature goose, take my advice and use it to make some Goose sausages (see p.202). They are a great use for this rich meat and freeze very well, giving you bangers and mash with a difference.

Goose meat makes for excellent burgers if you add an equal weight of smoked, fatty bacon to the goose flesh before mincing and shaping. Or you can use the mince to make a Gamekeeper's pie (see p.205).

Greylag *Anser anser*

NOMENCLATURE	Goose (*f*); gander (*m*); gosling (*young*); gaggle, paddling or flock (*group*); skein (*group in flight*)
CONSERVATION STATUS	Migratory or fluctuating population
HABITAT	Shoreline, estuaries, wetlands, farmland and marshland
HUNTING SEASON	1 Sept–31 Jan, extending to 20 Feb on the shoreline (England, Wales and Scotland); 1 Sept–31 Jan regardless of location (N Ireland)

The noble greylag is the largest of our native geese species, and its sheer size makes you wonder at its ability to fly at all, let alone to do it in style. But these are in fact the most graceful of geese, both on the water and in flight.

There are two types of greylag in the UK. The first are truly wild and you will only find them in Scotland, where they migrate to from Iceland in winter. The second is a semi-wild population probably originating from escapees from private collections on grand estates. These are present in the UK all year round, breeding on lakes and estuaries around the lowlands and along the coast.

Because of the different factors affecting the overall population, the number of these geese in the UK is thought to fluctuate between 50,000 and 200,000. However, there is little conservation concern for the greylag, be it truly wild and resident, migratory or from the more modern 'feral' populations around the UK.

In the kitchen

If you think about the wingspan of these birds, and the sheer strength needed to lift them into flight, it's not surprising that the breast muscle is somewhat chewy. And since they are swimming or walking whenever they're not flying around, it follows that the leg meat is even more so. Hanging time is therefore crucial. The longer you hang greylags, the more tender they become. But they also begin to go green (or off) quite quickly, even in the fridge, so a compromise is needed (see p.140).

You can slow-roast a whole greylag if you have the time to pluck it. This can be successful and delicious, but I have had mixed results with a seemingly young and tender bird being tough for no apparent reason. You have been warned.

Pink-footed goose *Anser brachyrhynchus*

NOMENCLATURE	Goose (*f*); gander (*m*); gosling (*young*); gaggle, paddling or flock (*group*); skein (*group in flight*)
CONSERVATION STATUS	Migratory or fluctuating population
HABITAT	Shoreline, coastal wetlands, salt marshes, rivers, lakes, ponds and farmland
HUNTING SEASON	1 Sept–31 Jan, extending to 20 Feb on the shoreline (England, Wales and Scotland); 1 Sept–31 Jan regardless of location (N Ireland)

This small goose which, as you may have guessed, has pink feet, arrives on our shores around October when its homelands of Greenland and Iceland start to get too chilly for it. One of the most impressive sights in nature is a massive paddling of these birds grouped together on the marsh. It's enough to take your breath away, especially when you consider the journey that they have made in order to get here.

The wild, unpredictable behaviour of the pink-footed goose makes it tricky to shoot, often requiring the hunter to head far from home and out into cold winter estuaries at dawn and dusk. Numbers are on the rise due to better hunting controls, both in their nesting sites abroad and here in the UK while they overwinter – a fine example of conservationists and hunters working together.

In the kitchen

These are tasty birds, on the whole: better and sweeter, I would say, than the larger geese on the menu. I don't recommend hanging them as they have a tendency to go green, or a bit high, verging on off, very quickly.

If you're lucky enough to get hold of a young, tender pink-footed goose, then roasting it whole is a good way to treat it. Season the bird well, place it on its back in a hot roasting tray and roast in a hot oven at 220°C/Gas mark 7 for 10 minutes. Turn it on to one side and give it another 6 minutes, then repeat on the other side. Now turn the bird breast side down and give it 5 minutes. To finish the cooking, turn off the oven but leave the bird inside for another 10 minutes before removing it. Allow it to rest for another 15 minutes before carving.

Slow-roasting is an effective way to tenderise a middle-aged pinkfoot, especially if you give it the soy and ginger treatment (see Slow-roast spiced soy duck, p.193).

With older geese, remove just the breasts and legs and use them for soups, stews or a Game curry (see p.240), or mince for a Gamekeeper's pie (see p.205) or a batch of Goose sausages (see p.202).

Deer

Venison is seriously tasty stuff. One species or another is in season all year round and, from a healthy eating point of view, deer meat is lower in fat and higher in protein than farmed meats, and has a broader spectrum of vitamins and minerals.

Deer fit into the category of wild meat I call 'accidentally farmed', because they thrive on the habitat we have created to grow crops in. They actually do a great deal of damage on farmland and in forests, which is one of the reasons the population needs to be managed (good news for the cook).

There are three main categories of deer in the UK: wild, 'parked' and farmed (as described overleaf). We also, inexplicably, import huge quantities of venison from abroad, including such far-flung places as New Zealand. Most venison meat sold in UK supermarkets is from British farms or parks, but do check.

For all deer species, and the different sexes of those species, except muntjac, there are strictly enforced open and closed seasons to protect the breeding cycle and ensure no dependent young are left to fend for themselves.

Identifying the different species can be a little tricky to start with, and seasonal changes in colour and appearance of the deer make things even more complex. But, with a modicum of study, you will be able to identify the species and their sex relatively quickly.

Young deer (fawns, kids or calves depending on the species) are born in the spring except for muntjac deer, which are quite happy breeding the year round. During the mating season, known as the rut, male deer scent themselves from special scent glands on their bodies and heads, and urinate in muddy areas then roll in this heady concoction. They also adorn their antlers with vegetation, roar at each other and often battle to establish territories and earn the right to the females (does or hinds) within that territory, though often it is the female who decides exactly who to mate with and when. Though these fights are seldom serious, they do occasionally escalate when two males are evenly matched, resulting in injury or even the death of one or both of them.

Male deer grow new antlers each season and the size of these and the number of their points is a sign of age, and also an indicator of food availability. No male deer can grow a decent 'head' (as the antlers are known) without sufficient nutrients to do so. When the antlers are growing they are covered in a soft, blood-filled tissue layer, called velvet.

Once the antlers are fully grown, the animal will 'fray' the velvet by rubbing their antlers on tree and bushes, as well as the ground. Sap released from trees and dirt colours the antlers, which would otherwise be white, as they are made of bone not horn. In the autumn, the antlers fall off and the whole process starts again, with new antlers growing from the two pedicles on the head of the deer.

A fallow doe in a deer sanctuary

Farmed deer

Fully farmed venison is produced by bringing in six-month-old deer from rearing parks across the country (mostly in Scotland) then 'finishing' them in an agricultural system. They are fed on hay, grain and cake pellets until they are the right weight for slaughter. They will also be wormed at intervals.

During their time on the farm the deer become used to humans and less inclined to stress and panic, allowing them, in theory at least, to be slaughtered in a specially designed abattoir in much the same way as pigs, sheep and cows. In practice, however, they are often shot in the grazing field because there are few deer abattoirs in existence. If undertaken by an experienced marksman with a rifle, I would consider this an acceptable manner of dispatch.

Deer are farmed in this way in order to provide a constant supply of venison to larger retailers and restaurants, which are often intent on having a 'consistent' product that hardly changes with the seasons. There is also a rising demand for venison in general. The deer farming industry is one way of meeting that demand and is a good example of low-impact, high-welfare farming.

Parked deer

The practice of building walls and fences to keep deer in one place dates back centuries. It made a lot of sense in years past: you always knew where your deer were and, in the days of widespread poaching and poverty (the first deer parks date back to the fifteenth century), being able to protect your herd was no small matter.

Deer parks quickly became prized possessions, gifted by the crown to people in its service, and the warrant to own a park was a most valuable asset. There are historical references to deer parks all over the country. Indeed, Park Farm – the site of River Cottage HQ – is so named because there used to be a deer park there. A few of the old ones are still in use, most notably Richmond Park in Surrey and Knole Park in Kent, with their red and fallow deer herds. However, a lot of venison these days comes from modern deer parks, such as Powderham in Exeter and Woburn in Bedfordshire – great places to watch deer displaying natural behaviour.

In a park, deer from the wild, or deer introduced from herds abroad, are kept on enclosed land where they behave as semi-wild animals and are allowed to breed. Selected animals are culled for meat. The deer become used to humans so they can be shot at close range with a rifle, usually in the head, meaning there is less damage to the carcass and the deer is instantly and humanely dispatched. Deer parking is also a way of managing the land on which the animals reside by keeping pasture and scrub well under control.

Meat from deer parks is of good quality and consistent throughout the year. Red, fallow and sika deer are all raised in parks, but if you want meat from the smaller species, such as roe, you will have to look elsewhere.

Wild deer

There are six species of deer living wild in the UK. They are red, fallow, sika, roe, muntjac and Chinese water deer. Only red and roe are truly native, although fallow have been here for such a long time, having arrived from Europe as early as the first century AD, that they are practically naturalised.

According to leading deer groups such as the British Deer Society (BDS), deer numbers in the UK are on an upward curve, meaning that, among other things, deer are moving into new territories all the time, often coming into conflict with people along the way. Deer-related road traffic accidents have been increasing year on year, and farmers and foresters are reporting record levels of deer damage to crops and growing timber. Though this is not an excuse for wholesale slaughter of these bewitching animals, it makes sense to manage the increasing population – and feed ourselves at the same time.

I am often asked if road-killed deer can be eaten. Caution is the best advice I can offer here. Personally, I wouldn't eat a deer knocked down by a car as there has been no opportunity to study its behaviour prior to the incident and therefore no way of assessing its health. There's a good chance it won't have died quickly and this too can cause problems with the meat. And unless you have been trained in eviscerating a deer – a process known as 'gralloching' – you won't know the telltale signs of disease or vermin damage.

All six species of deer are hunted in the UK at some point throughout the year and are obtained by stalking: the act of hunting deer with a rifle. It takes skill, patience, knowledge and a firearms certificate to go out and stalk deer in the wild and it is essential that you undertake some kind of formal training if you want to do it. The BDS offers fantastic courses in deerstalking, as do other organisations (see the Directory, p.248). Alternatively, you can get hold of some of this top-notch wild meat from a game dealer, or a friendly deerstalker.

For me, wild venison has the edge on flavour over parked or farmed meat. This is for the simple reason that wild deer tend to have a much more varied diet than their cultivated relations. The type of venison that you cook with will be determined primarily by local supply, but all of the recipes for venison in this book will work well with any species.

P.S. The vast majority of wild deer are not shot in the head, which would seem the obvious target. The BDS recommends heart and lung shots as these are more humane and offer less chance of injured deer escaping before they can be dispatched. In the preparation sequence on pp.158–163, the small roe deer has been heart and lung shot, though the shot placement isn't perfect. However, I have it on authority from the stalker who supplied it that it was still a fatal shot – a good illustration of why this is the recommended approach.

Comparative size of deer species (male)

Muntjac

Chinese water deer

Roe deer

Sika deer

Fallow deer

Red deer

| 0 | 50 | 100 | 150 | 200 |

Centimetres

A red deer stag and his hinds

Red deer *Cervus elaphus*

NOMENCLATURE	Hind (*f*); stag (*m*); calf (*young*); pricket (*juvenile male*); herd (*group*)
CONSERVATION STATUS	Abundant population, also farmed
HABITAT	Woodland, downland and highlands
HUNTING SEASON	Different for males and females; also varies according to location (see charts on pp.38–43)

The largest deer in the UK and one of only two truly native species, the red deer has stood as a symbol of wealth, honour, ownership and power for as long as there have been people around to hunt it. Often thought of as creatures of the hills and highlands, they are actually more at home in the forests and woods of the lowlands. In their preferred habitat red deer grow to a larger size and often have a better life than their open-hill-dwelling brothers and sisters, owing to the availability of food and year-round protection from the elements.

It is unlikely that you'll just happen upon a red deer, unless you're out on the hills of the Scottish Highlands, where you may well be able to see them grazing in the distance. And you don't really want to get up close to a fully grown adult in any case: these are big animals and the males, at least, are well equipped to do you some damage should you get too near. I have, on occasion, startled a red deer in thick woodland cover while out looking for mushrooms or, more occasionally, woodcock: it's a heart-stopping moment when this massive beast charges past with its shaggy head up, seeking the nearest exit. Red deer can weigh up to 120kg, which makes them very large wild animals to encounter up close.

As with all deer, to a greater or lesser extent, the hierarchy within red deer herds is constantly being challenged. As a result, there is seldom a dull moment, particularly during the rut, or breeding season, from September to October, when the stags daub themselves with a heady blend of mud, urine and excretions from their scent glands. They also adorn their impressive antlers with bracken, grass and other vegetation and then roar at each other to establish breeding rights. This often ends in confrontation and stags will fight each other in antler-clashing fury. This can cause serious injury or even death but, more often than not, the weaker stag submits and runs off before things get too heated.

Around May and June, red deer young will be born in a quiet, out-of-the-way place where the hind can be alone and feel safe. It was believed for a long time that deer were terrible mothers, but it's now understood that the young are left alone

A red deer hind

when they are most helpless in order to protect them. They have very little scent and can lie almost completely motionless for hours until the mother returns to feed them, clean them and then leave them alone again. This means they are left free of *her* scent – by which predators would be able to locate the young, defenceless animals. If you do find a calf or fawn on its own whilst out in the countryside, just leave it be.

In the kitchen

A whole adult red deer, or even a small hind or young pricket, presents quite a serious task of skinning and butchery and one that should not be undertaken lightly, or without at least some understanding of the job in hand. And, unless you have a very large family of a carnivorous nature, you are going to need a big freezer in which to store a lot of the meat.

If you do find yourself in possession of a whole deer in the fur, refer to the guide to hanging times on p.140; a week of hanging will be necessary in most cases. For butchery instructions, see the preparation guide on pp.158–167. Whenever I have a whole haunch (back leg) to deal with, I tend to break it down into separate muscles and divide these for use as smaller roasts or steaks. Roasting a haunch whole would be a tricky thing to do, as there are many different muscles in the one joint, some more tender than others and all low in fat – and you would need a big oven. The same applies to the saddle (back); from this I like to cut a few cutlets or chops as well.

I prefer to marinate my venison, and I always do so with an oil-based paste (see Herb marinade with star anise, p.223) rather than a liquid. Oils don't pickle the meat, as wine can, and have the added benefit of excluding air, which stops the meat oxidising and prolongs its life. Key flavours for me are star anise and black pepper; something about that combination of warmth and old-world aroma sits so well with venison. I often, but not always, add some 'hard' herbs, such as rosemary and thyme, and venison also goes very well with bay (cooked as for Roast saddle of hare with bay and sumac, see p.233).

A favourite way to savour a haunch steak is Venison with marrow pickle (see p.220). You can also use the haunch to make Spicy fajitas (see p.195) and fried crumb-coated escalopes (as for Wild boar Holstein, see p.226). Venison liver is also very good, especially if you serve it with a parsley and caper sauce, as in Venison liver persillade (see p.224).

If you're happy that your venison is fresh and clean, there can be few more enjoyable treats than a good plate of Venison carpaccio (see p.219).

A fallow doe

Fallow deer *Dama dama*

NOMENCLATURE	Doe (*f*); buck (*m*); fawn (*young*); herd (*group*)
CONSERVATION STATUS	Abundant population, also farmed
HABITAT	Parkland, woodland and farmland
HUNTING SEASON	Different for males and females; also varies according to location (see charts on pp.38–43)

Fallow deer are distributed across most of the UK, although they are rare in Scotland. They can be tricky to identify as they have a diverse range of colourings and markings that change with the seasons. They do, however, have quite long tails for deer and the male's antlers are 'palmate', with a sort of scoop-like webbing between points, much like those of a moose. Fallow deer are also smaller than red deer, but much larger than roe.

There are three distinct types of fallow deer: menial, common and melanistic. All are distinctly different in appearance, but taste much the same. Fallow are not native deer but were brought into the country by the Normans and kept as livestock. They still make up the vast majority of parked deer in the UK. This is because their carcasses are slightly easier to deal with than the big reds, but still have plenty of meat on them. This meat is also among the best of the large deer, only pipped to the post by the sika, which, for my money, has the best meat of all deer, large or small. Fallow deer's varied and beautiful pelts provide a useful secondary income for the deer park too, in the form of rugs, belts and clothing.

In the kitchen

You shouldn't have any trouble getting hold of fallow venison with just a little research. You'll rarely be far from a deer-park-ful and these days, of course, many of the more up-to-date deer parks sell their meat online.

If the fallow has come from a park it is likely to have been well fed and managed, and its tasty meat will probably have the added benefit of a little more fat than most venison. That in itself adds an extra dimension to the meat, which has a sweeter flavour and much smoother texture than red deer venison.

If you are dealing with a whole carcass you're going to need to think about storage, as these are pretty big animals, and a minimum hanging time of a week will be needed (see p.140) before skinning. Fallow venison is suitable for the following: Venison carpaccio (see p.219), Venison with marrow pickle (see p.220), Roast saddle of hare with bay and sumac (see p.233), Wild boar Holstein (see p.226), Spicy fajitas (see p.195) and Venison liver persillade (see p.224).

Sika deer *Cervus nippon*

NOMENCLATURE	Hind (*f*); stag (*m*); calf (*young*); herd (*group*)
CONSERVATION STATUS	Wild: locally sporadic population; farmed: abundant population
HABITAT	Parkland, woodland and farmland
HUNTING SEASON	Different for males and females; also varies according to location (see charts on pp.38–43)

These large deer come from Japan, as their Latin name indicates; *cervus* means 'stag' and *nippon* means 'Japanese'. The first Japanese sika deer in the UK arrived in 1860 and were a gift to London Zoo. More were sent to Ireland, where they were bred and then sold on to deer collectors in England. Shortly after this, a few wild colonies established themselves, thanks to deer either escaping or being set free.

Today there are a few different types of sika around. It's believed that these are either hybridised with red deer, or with another species of sika, called Manchurian (*Cervus nippon mantchuricus*). In any case, it's certainly true that sika can – and will – interbreed to some extent with red deer populations. It is for this reason that some Scottish islands have been set up as red deer reserves, with the intention of keeping some red deer blood lines free of the sika, although the effectiveness of this remains to be seen as sika are, like all deer, rather good swimmers.

Sika, in common with other deer, are difficult to stalk, as they generally prefer to keep hidden during daylight hours. The best sika identification mark is the wide white or pale-coloured V-shaped pattern above the eyes and below the antlers. The tail is longer than that of a red deer and shorter than that of a fallow but, unless you happen to have all three neatly lined up together, it can be tricky to judge this.

The rutting season for sika runs from September to early November, and it is marked by the call of the rutting stags – a distinctive, high-pitched squeak. The offspring will be born around June.

In the kitchen

Dealing with a whole carcass will take time and planning, as well as a big freezer. Hanging in the fur should be for around a week at a stable temperature (see p.140).

Sika is, in my view, the best of the venison. Richer than red deer, it often carries plenty of fat, and is very tender given the size of the beast. The following recipes all work well: Venison carpaccio (see p.219), Venison with marrow pickle (see p.220), Roast saddle of hare with bay and sumac (see p.233), Wild boar Holstein (see p.226), Spicy fajitas (see p.195) and Venison liver persillade (see p.224).

A sika stag

A roe doe

Roe deer *Capreolus capreolus*

NOMENCLATURE	Doe (*f*); buck (*m*); kid or fawn (*young*); herd (*group*)
CONSERVATION STATUS	Abundant population
HABITAT	Woodland and farmland
HUNTING SEASON	Different for males and females; also varies according to location (see charts on pp.38–41); none of this species in N Ireland

From time to time, you will see roe deer creeping up the edge of woodlands around dawn and dusk. If you get the chance to watch them, take it. They seem to appear out of nowhere and are truly enchanting: you get the sense you are witnessing something very special and ancient, almost atavistic – as if you've been transported back in time. For me, there is a modicum of this feeling when I spot any deer, but it is strongest with roe deer. You can also often hear them barking to one another in the woods, particularly around the hours of sunrise and twilight. Sadly, however, most roe deer encounters are in the car and it's usually an unhappy meeting for at least one party, often both.

The rut for roe deer is July to August, but the kids, or fawns, are not born until May, due to the roe's extremely impressive ability to delay the implantation of fertile eggs into the womb. This clever trick allows the female deer to wait and see what the conditions are like and how much food is around before committing to the pregnancy. If the conditions then worsen, the doe is able to abort the pregnancy and re-absorb the vital nutrients to help keep her well and fertile for the next breeding cycle.

In the kitchen

If I acquire a whole roe deer, I don't tend to hang it for more than a day or two as this small deer simply doesn't need any longer (see p.140).

The meat from roe deer is superb, but care must be taken when cooking the tender meat (steaks and chops), as resting the rare cuts for too long can result in the meat taking on a strange, grainy texture. So keep an eye on your timings and if people are late for supper, start without them.

Venison carpaccio (see p.219), Venison with marrow pickle (see p.220), Roast saddle of hare with bay and sumac (see p.233), Wild boar Holstein (see p.226), Spicy fajitas (see p.195) and Venison liver persillade (see p.224) all work well with roe venison.

Muntjac *Muntiacus reevesi*

NOMENCLATURE	Doe (*f*); buck (*m*); fawn (*young*); herd (*group*)
CONSERVATION STATUS	Abundant population
HABITAT	Woodland, farmland, suburban gardens and parks
HUNTING SEASON	No closed season

Thought to be the most prolific deer in the UK, the muntjac is not native to this land. It was introduced in the early twentieth century to parks and some of them made their way into the wild from there. In all probability, more muntjac live close to humans than any other species. They are colonising suburbia at an astonishing rate. Like roe deer, they are territorial and mark their territories with scent, protecting their patch with aggression if need be.

These very small deer have tusks, in common with Chinese water deer, as well as antlers. They also have a long tail, which helps to distinguish them from small roe deer. Uniquely among deer species in the UK, muntjac have a modern approach to relationships, with the male often staying with the female for much of the time and helping with the family chores. Indeed, shared grooming is not uncommon.

Muntjac meat is excellent and there is currently no closed season because they breed all year round (closed seasons are in place for other species to protect the young before they are able to fend for themselves). Hunters should, therefore, be careful not to take muntjac with dependent young at foot. Many farmers and foresters see muntjac as pests, so the meat is relatively easy to get hold of in areas where muntjac are present in reasonable numbers.

In the kitchen

These small deer are very easy to handle if you follow the skinning and preparation guide on pp.158–167. I don't hang muntjac for very long at all – a day or so will be fine, though once skinned and jointed a few more days in the fridge will improve the meat a little.

Because of the muntjac's small size, its meat can be cooked more quickly than most. It is ideal for a barbecue and a whole muntjac – either jointed or spit-roasted – will feed around 15 people. The meat has a mild, almost veal-like taste that suits delicate dishes, but it's also good in the following recipes: Venison carpaccio (see p.219), Venison with marrow pickle (see p.220), Roast saddle of hare with bay and sumac (see p.233), Wild boar Holstein (see p.226), Spicy fajitas (see p.195) and Venison liver persillade (see p.224).

A muntjac doe

Chinese water deer *Hydropotes inermis*

NOMENCLATURE	Doe (*f*); buck (*m*); fawn (*young*); herd (*group*)
CONSERVATION STATUS	Sporadic population, mostly in eastern England, where it can be prolific
HABITAT	Woodland, farmland, suburban gardens and parks
HUNTING SEASON	1 Nov–31 Mar (England and Wales); none of this species in Scotland or N Ireland

A Chinese water deer looks rather like a cross between a marsupial teddy bear and a vampire. These small, elusive deer tend to be larger at the back than the front, like a kangaroo on all fours, and have very apparent small tusks. They are easily distinguishable from the similarly tusked muntjac, as the males lack antlers and their tusks are longer (the female's tusks are smaller than the male's).

Chinese water deer were first kept at London Zoo in 1873, but the wild population started with escapees from Whipsnade Zoo, where they had been introduced in 1929. This population rapidly spread to surrounding areas of friendly habitat, and their numbers are still on the rise, with an estimated wild population of over 2,000 today.

Male Chinese water deer rut in December, using their long tusks to establish a hierarchy and attract the attention of desirable females. The resulting young are born the following June or July. Chinese water deer are very good at breeding and can give birth to up to seven fawns at once, but infant mortality is high, with up to 40% of fawns dying within a fortnight of birth.

In the kitchen

The meat of the Chinese water deer is among the best venison. Requiring only a day or two of hanging (see p.140), it is sweet and rich, with a distinctive gamey edge that sets it apart from muntjac.

It works well in the following recipes: Venison carpaccio (see p.219), Venison with marrow pickle (see p.220), Roast saddle of hare with bay and sumac (see p.233), Wild boar Holstein (see p.226), Spicy fajitas (see p.195) and Venison liver persillade (see p.224). The haunch and neck meat also make excellent kebabs, served with flatbreads, harissa and salad.

A Chinese water deer buck

Buying &
Preparing Game

Buying game

Not everyone will have a ready supply of fresh game. If you are more likely to be buying than shooting, I'd like to offer you some advice on sourcing and obtaining the best possible game, and show you what to look for in terms of quality.

Firstly, a word on poaching. Poachers may seem affable enough but, since they clearly have a complete disregard for the law, as well as other people's property, I'd be deeply sceptical about how much care they will have taken with their ill-gotten gains. More to the point, if they are not supposed to be hunting where they are, will they be in possession of all the necessary facts? For example, is the farmer or gamekeeper on that ground using poison for squirrels or rats – poison that may have contaminated the meat? Is there TB in the deer herd? Buyer beware: I would urge you to do as I do and only buy game from people you know and trust.

There can be no substitute for buying game from a first-class butcher's shop or reputable game dealer. In both cases, all the hard work will be done for you – so no feathers, fur or innards to deal with. You will pay a little more at the butcher's shop, as the meat will most likely have been purchased ready-prepared from a game dealer, but in return you will probably get good service. A decent butcher will guide you through what they have, discuss what else they can get for you and should be happy to do any further meat preparation for you (provided they have the time – giving them a little notice is always a good thing).

You will also be able to get top-quality birds and beasts from a good local game dealer, but you may find them a bit harder to interact with. Most are focused on selling game in wholesale quantities and, if you catch them when they are very busy, you may find they are less than attentive.

These days you can, of course, buy game online from quite a few sources and they will deliver your meat, in chilled packaging, via a courier. If you find the right company, this is a good option. But, as always, a little research pays off. It's often worth telephoning rather than ordering direct from the site – even if you only do this the first time – to make sure you have the details correct. For example, I would insist on hen pheasants if I were planning a roast (see p.171). A phone call also gives the supplier a chance to offer advice as needed.

Many supermarkets now stock game in season, with venison, rabbit, pigeon and wild boar being available all year round. Check the origin though, as much venison is imported and farmed rabbit and pigeon should be avoided.

The other option is to get in touch with a local shoot or trained hunter, visit them after a shoot and choose your own birds or beasts, in the feather or fur. This is undoubtedly the least expensive option. It also gives you the opportunity to select the very best animals from the day's shooting and to build a relationship with your local game producers.

The illustrated guides on pp.146–167 take you through the whole process of preparing game. For a more hands-on approach, you might prefer to take a game preparation and cookery course; see the Directory, p.249 for a list of providers.

If you want to give away or share game meat you have shot yourself, you are perfectly entitled to do so. However, if you wish to sell or barter your meat to a butcher's shop or restaurant, then the carcass must be inspected by a trained hunter to ensure it's fit for human consumption. Both the British Association for Shooting and Conservation (BASC) and the British Deer Society (BDS) run training courses (see the Directory, p.248).

Birds

If you want tender, moist birds, then you need the younger ones. Early on in the season, size is a good indicator: smaller birds are likely to be this year's brood.

Feel the breasts of the bird as it hangs: don't buy anything that isn't a little plump and firm as this indicates it has yet to reach its prime, or indeed may have struggled to put on weight, possibly indicating poor health. Use your hands to assess whether the bird has lots of broken bones, suggesting a fall from a great height or possibly bad dog work during retrieval.

Later in the season (i.e. past mid-November), all birds tend to be a similar size because the new brood will have caught up with last year's. In this case, feel the legs: are they horny and hard to the touch? Or smooth and soft, indicating a younger bird? Feel a few to get a good comparison and help you make a judgement. Avoid birds that have been overly damaged by shot, or at least barter a better price for these specimens. You may even find you can get them for nothing.

Don't worry about age with birds like woodcock or snipe, just be glad you can get them at all. The age of ducks is easy enough to assess, by trying to tear the webbing between the claws – the softer this is and the more easily it tears, the younger the bird. The same applies to geese and you can also attempt to bend the bill, the more easily it bends the younger the bird.

Small furred game

It's a little harder to judge age with rabbits and hare but, particularly with rabbits, go for smaller ones. Always have a look at the eyes. Fresh game should look fresh, even if it has started the process of rigor mortis: eyes should be bright and shiny, not sunken or dry-looking.

Ideally, look for head-shot rabbits and hares, taken with a small-bore rifle. Those taken with a shotgun tend to get badly bruised and can be a pain to prepare. Ferreted rabbits are another good option. In all cases, look at the coat of the animal. In wet weather, it's normal for them to look a little bedraggled, but avoid any that look sickly, overly damaged or particularly dirty.

Venison

Venison, of any type, should be available with just a few days' notice, depending upon the season. But make sure you specify exactly what you want when ordering, i.e. farmed/parked or wild deer, your preferred species and, of course, the specific cuts you would like. I would always also check that the venison you order is from the UK; many butchers and supermarkets sell imported meat from as far away as New Zealand.

You want to see that the carcass is hanging in a suitable place such as a large, walk-in fridge or cold, clean barn area. If the deer is hanging outside, exposed to the elements, or in an old shed with dirt and straw and old paint tins knocking about the place, it's probably best avoided. Make sure the carcass is fresh and not green or discoloured, and that it looks dry and clean inside the body cavity. A few ticks on the fur are normal and it's not at all unusual for the fur to have a lot of mud or dirt on it, but this should be on the outside, not within the body cavity.

It is quite common for the shoulder area of the animal to have a lot of damage from a bullet wound, but excessive damage should be taken into account when agreeing a price.

If you are in any doubt about the safety of the meat or the legitimate origin of the carcass, don't buy it. Most qualified hunters will attach a tag to the carcass with their registration number on and a few details such as their name, where the deer was shot and when, approximate weight, sex and species.

Buying prepared game

There is one disadvantage to buying your game meat ready-prepared (plucked, boned, gutted etc.), which is that you won't be able to assess the whole animal for signs of freshness and age. On the other hand, you will easily be able to see if the bird or animal has been 'hard-shot' (meaning it has been heavily hit in the body by the pellets, causing more than normal damage). Removal of skin and feathers makes such things far more obvious.

When choosing prepared game, all you have to do is apply the same rules you would when buying farmed meat. It may well come wrapped in plastic but if you can buy it 'open', I'd recommend this. It means the skin will be nice and dry and you can see the texture. Make sure the meat has no obvious signs of serious damage. It's not at all unusual to see some discoloration, particularly around the area where the guts have been removed, and game will smell stronger than other meats, due to its very nature, but it certainly shouldn't smell bad or appear green and slimy.

Again, I would recommend avoiding the biggest birds and animals (though it may be tempting to do otherwise as they are nearly always sold by number rather than weight). Larger animals will almost certainly be older and, therefore, tougher.

Hanging

Meat is hung to tenderise it and develop the flavour. Hanging is, in reality, the slow and controlled decomposition of the animal. Traditionally game birds and animals are hung in a cool place where air can circulate around them for quite a long time – often a couple of weeks. Birds are hung with guts in and animals with guts out, except for hare. Enzymes within the flesh begin to break down the muscle and connective tissues, making the meat more tender and allowing flavour the to develop. But this may not always be a good thing. I favour shorter periods of hanging – sometimes none at all – as this leaves the meat sweeter and fresher and I prefer the sweetness of very fresh game to the tenderness of well-hung, stronger-tasting meat. For example, I often eat birds on the day they are shot, once they've passed through rigor mortis (the natural stiffening and then loosening of the carcass after death).

Primary hanging

There are two types of hanging: hanging in the fur or feather (primary hanging) and hanging after preparation (secondary hanging) in order to further age the meat. This secondary process only really applies with larger game such as wild boar and venison.

Prior to primary hanging, the carcass must be allowed to cool down completely but quickly. All too often, for instance, shot birds are loaded up in the back of a truck and left until the end of the day. Piled together like this, or stuffed in a game bag, they don't cool quickly and, as a result, bacterial multiplication is much more rapid. The same is true with rabbits, which should be laid out on the cool ground, or hung up in a cool place, as soon after gutting as possible. Venison carcasses should be hung in a cool place soon after gralloching (the removal of the viscera).

Any game that is badly damaged, or particularly wet or dirty, should not be hung at all because it is likely to go off (or green) in a very short time. It should be prepared for cooking as soon as it has cooled.

With birds, it makes little difference which way up you hang them as the viscera are left in. Generally, game birds are tied together in braces before being hung up.

Larger mammals should be hung head down to allow any residual blood to drip out. Metal hooks will need to be passed between the tendon and bone of the lower leg to allow hanging.

Temperature is the most important consideration in the primary hanging environment. If you are able to control the temperature, by hanging your game in a walk-in fridge that can be maintained at 4–6°C, for instance, so much the better. If you hang your game in a shed or garage and the temperature is uncontrolled and fluctuating, then things get a little more complicated and here you will have to use

Primary hanging times

	GAME TYPE	MAXIMUM TIME AT 4–6°C (COLD)	MAXIMUM TIME AT 4–10°C (FLUCTUATING)	MAXIMUM TIME AT 8–12°C (WARM)
FEATHERED	Pheasant	4 days in feather	2 days	1 day
	Wood pigeon	3 days in feather	2 days	1 day
	Rook	3 days in feather	2 days	1 day
	Woodcock	3 days in feather	2 days	1 day
	Snipe	3 days in feather	2 days	1 day
	Duck	4 days in feather	2 days	1 day
	Teal	3 days in feather	2 days	1 day
	Goose	6 days in feather	3 days	2 days
FURRED	Hare	5 days in fur	2–3 days	36 hours
	Rabbit	4 days in fur	2 days	1 day
	Squirrel	3 days in fur	2 days	1 day
	Small deer	6 days in fur	3 days	2 days
	Large deer	7 days in fur	4 days	2 days
	Wild boar	7 days in fur	3 days	2 days

your judgement. For example, if I hang a few birds in the garage in early September and the weather is mild, they would probably spoil within a few days. However, if I hung them in the same place during an exceptionally cold January, and the temperature barely got above freezing, I could leave them for a week.

Secondary hanging

Larger game, such as boar and venison, can be aged by secondary hanging. You can also 'age on' wild geese or ducks for stews or pies with a greater depth of flavour. Secondary hanging takes place after the animal has been skinned or plucked and gutted and, in the case of boar or deer, butchered down into primal cuts (see pp.160–3). Any small or damaged cuts should be used immediately but larger cuts such as haunches or saddles can be hung back up in a fridge and aged for longer to develop the flavour and make the meat more tender (those enzymes at work again).

I wouldn't hesitate to hang a haunch of venison for another week or longer, providing there is a good amount of fat, or 'cover', on the meat (otherwise it will dry out too much and too quickly). Secondary hanging is also called dry-ageing because the meat gives up moisture to the air as it matures (not to be confused with dry-curing, which is a preserving method).

Dry-ageing is much used by butchers and chefs to improve the flavour and tenderness of beef cuts such as rib eye or sirloin. It often results in a dry, sticky, sometimes slightly mouldy layer forming on the outside of the meat. This is no cause for concern but should be trimmed off before further butchery and cooking. For dry-ageing you need a big fridge in which to hang cuts so that air can circulate around them. Otherwise, you'll just have to get on and butcher your meat down straight away before most likely storing it in the freezer.

Storage after hanging

After you have hung your game, you will have to decide whether to eat it straight away or store it. If you're planning on storing it, you have three options. You can store it in the fridge and use it within a few days, or freeze it, or you can preserve it by curing, air-drying or cooking.

In the fridge
If you are going to refrigerate your prepared game, it's best to keep it in airtight containers. I use sturdy plastic tubs with clip-on lids, but ceramic and glass dishes, tightly covered, are fine too. The exception to this is whole birds, which benefit from a little air circulation, as it helps to keep them dry. I still put them in a plastic container, but I tend to leave the lid off, or just cover the tub with a clean tea towel. Stored in this way, most fresh small game will keep well for 5 days or even longer, but keep an eye out and use up any that start to deteriorate first.

You can store boned, skinned game meat rubbed with a little oil and/or cure to help prolong its freshness (see p.199). The meat will continue to develop a bit but it won't dry out further and should be used within a few days.

In all cases, store raw meat on the lowest shelf of the fridge, so no juices can drip on to other foods.

Freezing
When it comes to freezing, your arch-enemy is air. Water will crystallise out of any pockets of air that are in contact with frozen meat and cause 'freezer burn', i.e. discoloured, dry patches that ruin the meat. I highly recommend a vacuum-packer, as this limits the chances of freezer burn and helps to make the most of the freezer space available. Domestic vacuum-packers are available at a reasonable price. If you do not have one, make sure you exclude as much air as you can and double-wrap any packages of game for the freezer. Remember to clearly label and date what you freeze too, so you can be sure to use the oldest items first. I also like to make a note on the label of where the animal was from.

There are few simpler ways to extend the life of your meat than by batch cooking it into stews and sauces and freezing these in convenient quantities, to be defrosted whenever you want a tasty meal in next to no time. Remember to label and date your differing batches so you can be sure to use the oldest up first, and so you can tell what it is later on – bags of frozen brown stuff all look the same.

Curing, air-drying, smoking and cooking

If you fancy trying something a little more traditional, air-drying, curing and smoking can be very delicious ways to preserve game. Hot-smoking and quick-curing are straightforward and are outlined in the recipes on pp.200, 243 and 199.

Preparing a whole carcass

Registered game dealers are controlled by law in much the same way as any butcher, fishmonger or restaurant. Records are kept of where each animal comes from, and the processes of skinning or plucking, eviscerating, chilling, packing and storing are all regulated by strict guidelines to protect public health.

If you are undertaking your own meat preparation, you will need to be your own regulator. It makes sense to establish a procedure and to have an understanding of the potential hazards and how to avoid them, so you can enjoy your game without any worries.

With any raw meat, there is always a risk of various forms of contamination, either from outside or inside the animal. A little of either is unavoidable but the risks must be controlled because the higher the level of contamination, the greater the chances of problems, such as food poisoning, occurring. You might find a few feathers clinging to a chicken bought at the butcher's, for instance, and some traces of the innards as well. But you wouldn't want to buy a bird with lots of blood and guts on the meat as this indicates that bacteria have had plenty of opportunity to multiply. Bacteria love blood and damaged flesh. The same goes for home-prepared carcasses.

Commonly occurring contaminants include:
- Dirt, mud and grit from the outside of the animal (on skin, feathers, feet)
- Potentially hazardous surface water from the animal's habitat
  (water-borne bacteria/viruses)
- Gut enzymes and bacteria from the inside of the animal's viscera
- Faecal matter from the digestive tract of the animal
- Blood from the animal
- Physical contamination from shot/bullets

Less common and potentially more difficult to deal with:
- Transmittable diseases, such as bird flu and TB (usually spotted by the hunter or on inspection of the carcass)
- Physical or chemical contamination, from pesticides or poisons (unlikely if the animals are being shot legally)
- Parasitic contamination, notably ticks passing on Lyme disease (any tick bites should be watched for a reaction and a doctor consulted if necessary)

So, your main aim when preparing game – or any meat – is to keep it as clean as possible and remove any parts that are particularly prone to contamination, such as heavily damaged muscle, the gut, head and feet. You should also ensure there is no contact between the raw meat and other foods, and that all equipment, and your work area, is cleaned very thoroughly both before and after use. Don't let any of this put you off – just treat your wild meat with care. Correct preparation, storage and cooking will reduce the risk of contamination to a minimum, in much the same way as it is reduced at the abattoir or your local butcher's shop.

You should follow a clearly defined process every time you deal with a carcass. The basic principles are the same for any game, except that you should pluck or skin a bird *before* removing the guts (see p.146), whereas with four-legged creatures, except hare, the guts need to be removed first; this is always done in the field at the time of dispatch or shortly after. If the carcass is not fresh from the field, it must be chilled to prevent decay from setting in too swiftly. I always store furred and feathered game in a separate fridge from prepared game, to ensure there can be no cross-contamination from the unprepared game to the prepared. I have a spare fridge in my garage for this purpose, which is left switched off when not in use.

Equipment
You will need a washable stout table and a few items of equipment to prepare and butcher a carcass but these needn't be expensive. The minimum you will need is:

- At least two stout chopping boards
- A small meat cleaver, or large chopping knife
- A meat saw, for larger animals
- A good plastic-handled, stainless-steel boning knife
- A butcher's sharpening steel
- Some decent kitchen scissors, strong enough to cut safely through the wing bones of birds
- Butcher's string
  Cleaning materials, including sanitiser spray, cloths and kitchen paper
  Sturdy bin bags

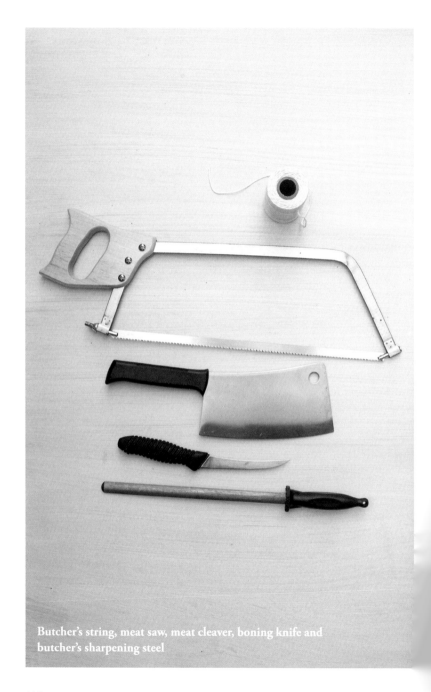

Butcher's string, meat saw, meat cleaver, boning knife and butcher's sharpening steel

Good procedure

Before making a start, ensure all surfaces and equipment are clean and dry. With clean and dry hands, check the animal over. Look for signs of poor health, such as large spots on the liver, kidneys or lungs, and/or swollen, runny eyes or a slimy nose. If any of these are present, I would recommend disposal of the carcass as this indicates illness or a high worm burden, though you may just need to discard the damaged or infected area such as the liver in mild cases.

- Assess the damage done during the dispatch of the animal. If, for example, a rabbit has been rifle-shot in the head, there is nothing to worry about as the head will be discarded. If the animal has been accidentally shot through the stomach, leg or shoulder, there may be debris from the guts or shards of bone in the meat. Cut out and discard any parts too damaged or spoilt to eat, before they can come into contact with the rest of the carcass or your clean meat prep board. If you are preparing a batch of game, it makes sense to use the more damaged birds or animals first, as they are likely to go off faster.

- Working on a board, carefully remove the skin, head and paws (see pp.154–7), or pluck the bird and remove the head and feet (see pp.146–9). Then remove everything from your work area (skin, feathers, cloth, knife, board etc.). If the carcass seems dirty, furry or has faecal matter on it, either give it a good wash in cold water or a wipe-down with a solution of one part cider vinegar to four parts water. In either case, dry it with a clean tea towel or kitchen paper, then place the carcass on a clean chopping board. Wash and dry your hands.

- Remove any remaining offal (lungs, heart etc.) from the ribcage. Check that the offal looks bright, clean and free from abnormal growths. Don't be too concerned about your animal if you find traces of liver damage, but don't eat the liver or kidneys as they are unlikely to taste good. If you find significant abnormal growths on the flesh or within the offal, discard the carcass.

- Rinse the carcass to ensure it is clean. You can now cut the meat up or leave it whole, as you like. Then you can either cook it or store it (see p.141).

- Thoroughly wash and dry all your equipment before you put it away.

Use a bit of common sense, employ some careful planning and put in a little practice and you will soon be proficient at preparing your own carcasses safely. The more you do it, the quicker and more confident you will become.

Plucking and gutting a bird

I like to pluck birds outside if at all possible to keep any feathery mess out of the house. It's also best to be seated, I think, as this stops you rushing the job – even the most momentary lack of attention can lead to torn skin.

- Holding the bird firmly in one hand, start plucking the feathers along the back, 3 or 4 at a time. Hold the feathers firmly in a two-finger-and-thumb pinch and pull them briskly away from the bird, drawing them directly from where they join the skin (see right). Keep a firm grip on the bird, placing your hand close to the area you are plucking; if you do tear the skin, this should stop the tear running too far. Work across the breasts and down the legs (pic 1, p.148).

- Continue until the feathers on the body are all gone. Don't bother to pluck the wings, neck or head as these will be discarded (pic 2).

- Remove the head and wings with a stout knife or kitchen scissors (pic 3).

- Remove the feet and the sinew from the legs at the same time (especially with pheasant). Begin by using the back of a knife to break the bone just below the ankle joint then bend the foot through 90° and rotate it three times to free the tendons. Holding the foot and leg firmly, pull one from the other (pic 4). The tendons should then come away with the foot of the bird. This should make the legs far more tender and enjoyable to eat. Trim off the ankle joints.

- To remove the guts, begin by making a small incision through the skin at the rear end of the bird (pic 5). Be careful not to stir the guts with the knife as that will cause unnecessary mess and possibly spoil the meat.

- Push the first two fingers of your hand into this small cut and run them along the underside of the breasts inside the cavity of the bird. Hook them over the whole parcel of guts and offal contained therein (pic 6).

- Gently pull out the guts (pic 7) and discard (keep the liver and heart if wished).

- Finally trim out the anus (pic 8) and check that the crop (a small, sticky white sac, which may or may not be full of food) is removed from the front of the breasts. Any remaining tiny feathers or down on the bird can easily be removed by briefly playing the flame of a cook's blowtorch over the surface of the skin, taking care not to char it. Rinse the carcass to ensure it is clean.

Plucking and gutting a bird

Boning a bird without plucking or gutting

Plucking and dressing birds in the traditional way (as described and shown on pp.146–9) can be time-consuming and is not always appropriate – when you have lots of birds to prepare and little time, for instance, or when the birds are too old or damaged to be used for roasting whole. In such circumstances, I always use the following method of preparation.

- With the bird lying breast up and head away from you on a chopping board, make a small cut in the skin by pinching the skin and feathers on top of the breasts and piercing with the tip of a knife (see right). Push a finger through the hole in the skin (pic 1, p.152).

- Holding the bird firmly on the other side, pull your finger sideways to expose the breast meat (pic 2).

- Push the legs forward whilst holding the skin back to expose the leg meat. Make sure you pull the skin all the way down to the feet (pic 3) to avoid wasting meat when you cut them off.

- Slice the breast meat off the carcass by cutting along the edge of the breast bone, which is easily visible between the two breasts. Then carefully cut along the wishbone. Now simply keep cutting until the breast is removed from the bone (pic 4), taking care not to cut into the internal cavity of the bird and into the guts. Repeat this process for the other breast.

- Removing the legs is a little trickier. Begin by pushing the leg back past the body to pop the ball and socket joint in the hip. Take care when doing this in case the thigh bone is broken; if it is, there will be very sharp bone shards inside the leg. Then cut through the flesh, between the ball and socket joint, with the knife (pic 5).

- Chop the foot and feathers off the leg (pic 6).

- Separate the thigh meat from the leg meat by simply cutting through the knuckle of the knee joint (pic 7).

- I keep the legs, saving them up in the freezer until I have enough to make a big batch of stew. (I pick the bones and sinew out of the stew before serving.) The thighs are best boned and used as you would a chicken thigh (pic 8).

Boning a bird without plucking or gutting

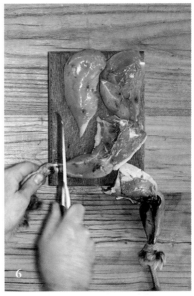

Skinning and butchering a rabbit

Follow the technique described and illustrated here to skin and butcher a rabbit or hare. A squirrel can be prepared in the same way.

- Begin by separating the skin from the meat on the open edge of the belly where the guts have been removed (see right). This will allow you to quickly make a loose flap of skin all the way around the rabbit (pic 1, p.156).

- Now pass a knife through between the carcass and the skin and cut outwards through the skin (pic 2) to divide the skin in two.

- Hold one half of the rabbit firmly at the head end and firmly pull away the fur from the other end, until you get to the feet (pic 3).

- Now hold the other end of the rabbit and firmly pull the fur from the head end (pic 4).

- Using a small meat cleaver or stout knife, chop off the furry feet, head and front paws (pic 5).

- Pull out the kidneys and remove any remaining offal from the ribcage. Make a cut into the pelvis bone between the hind legs on the inside of the carcass and, avoiding the now very sharp bones, remove the end of the intestines and any faecal matter therein, along with the bladder if it is still in place (pic 6). Rinse the carcass well.

- Cut the front end and the haunches from the saddle using a knife (pic 7) and a cleaver if needed. Trim the belly flaps and rib bones from the saddle with a pair of scissors.

- Split the haunches with a stout knife or cleaver, straight down the middle along the spine, and your task is complete (pic 8).

Skinning and butchering a rabbit

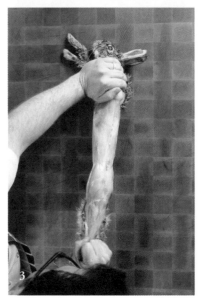

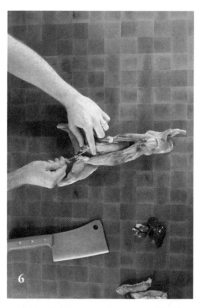

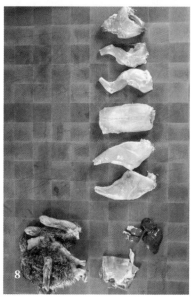

Skinning and butchering a deer

Follow the technique described and illustrated here to skin and butcher a deer. A wild boar can be prepared in the same way. Suspend the deer safely from the hind legs, making sure you can move freely around it. The carcass is best suspended by a gambrel on hooks from a beam, by attaching the hooks through the ankle tendons. If the feet have been cut off, then you will need to bind the legs to the hooks with rope, string or stout cable ties to ensure the deer won't fall down as you work.

Skinning

- Starting at the point where the back leg meets the belly area, use your hands to pull the skin away from the flesh up towards the foot end of the leg; go as far as you can. Then work a sharp knife in under the skin and cut outwards so you are slitting the skin. Repeat this process almost to the foot, creating an open seam all the way along the leg – be careful not to cut the tendons from which the meat is hanging. Then repeat this process on the other leg. Pull the skin down and away from the meat on each leg with a firm, even pressure (pic 1), freeing the skin from the meat with the knife where needed (akin to pulling down a sock).

- When you reach the tail you will need to cut between the vertebrae with the knife. Continue to pull the skin downwards, taking care to avoid pulling off any flesh with the skin and working around the back and sides of the carcass. Just keep in mind that you are basically peeling the skin off, starting at the top and working down; only use the knife to separate the connective tissues between the meat and the skin when needed (pic 2).

- When you get to the top of the shoulders, slit the skin down the front of the shoulders and peel it back (pic 3), employing the same technique you used on the back legs. Then pull the remaining skin from the carcass, ending with the neck.

- Wash or wipe down the carcass as needed to remove excess hair and blood. This can be done with a hose if you are in a suitable location, or you can wipe it down with clean cloths and a water-vinegar solution. If you opt for the hose you will need to let the carcass dry off for an hour or two (pic 4) before proceeding to butcher it. Before moving the carcass to the preparation area, check yourself carefully for ticks – it's not unknown for them to move from the deer skin to the butcher!

Butchering a deer into primal cuts

The instructions here will work just as well for wild boar as they do for deer. Ensure the preparation area is clean and you have all the equipment you require to hand. You will need a saw, boning knife, string and a knife sharpener, as well as trays and tubs for storage and a bin for waste.

- First, by cutting around the bone and then sawing through it, remove the very top of the neck, as this often has dirt and bits of fur on it (see right). Cut off the feet and leg ends to get rid of any remaining fur (pic 1, p.162).

- Now remove the shoulders. There won't be any bones to cut through as they are held to the side of the animal by muscle and sinew. Simply lift the shoulder by the end of the front leg and cut the connective tissues, moving the knife back around the shoulder blade and bringing it out by the neck (pic 2).

- Separate the saddle and haunches. First find the spot where the pelvis bone projects from the spine. Slice straight down on to the spine with the knife, then use the saw to cut through the spine (pic 3). Switch back to the knife to continue the cutting of the meat on the other side until you are all the way through the carcass.

- Remove the top of the neck from the saddle using the knife and saw (pic 4).

- Mark a line with the knife along the ribs approximately halfway down the horizontal of the carcass, taking into account any bullet damage, then saw along this line to separate the breast from the saddle (pic 5). Repeat on the other side of the carcass – this is the hardest of all the cuts required as sawing through the flexible rib bones can be tricky. Take your time and be careful – if the saw slips at this point you don't want to end up with a nasty cut.

- Cut and saw off the neck section at the point about midway down where the shoulders were (pic 6). If there's excessive damage, discard this piece or cut off the damaged parts and reserve the good meat for mincing, braising or dicing.

- Use the knife and saw to separate the haunches, simply cutting straight down along the spine (pic 7).

- You have now divided the deer into primal cuts (pic 8). Where you go from here depends on what you want from the carcass (steaks, stewing meat etc.). Put any damaged joints, with excess blood or bruising, aside for trimming.

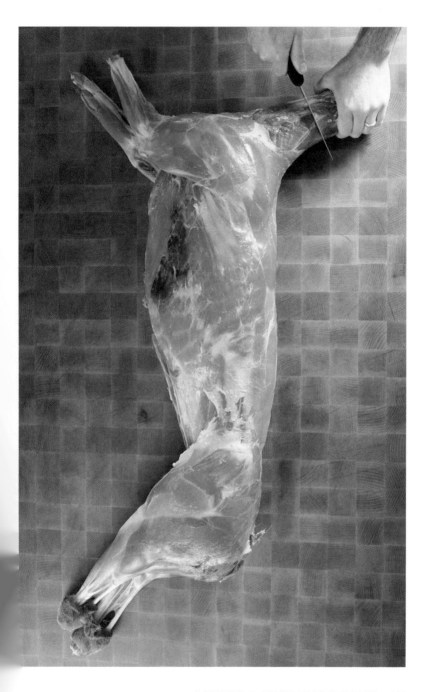

Butchering a deer into primal cuts

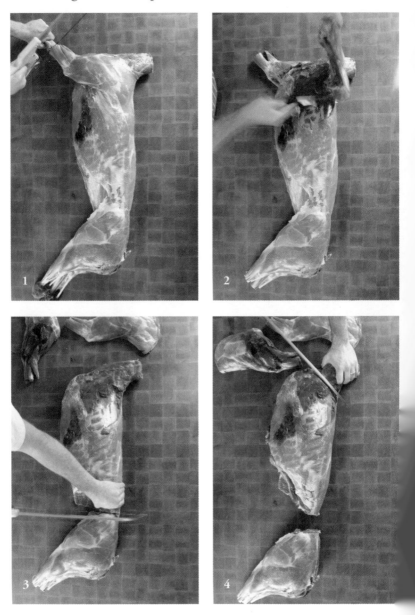

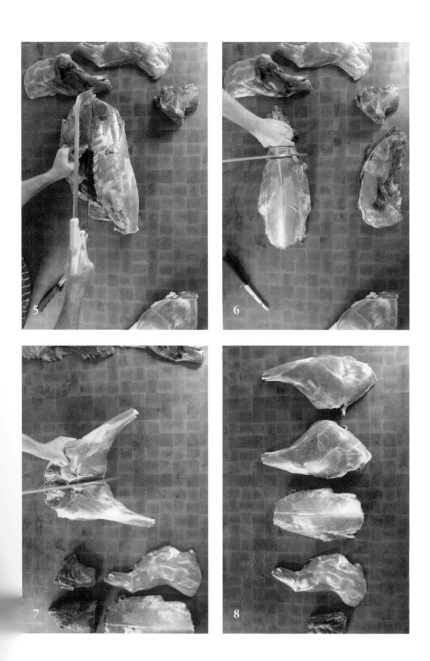

Further butchering a deer

How you decide to butcher your meat is very much a personal choice: this is how I do it. These instructions will work for any large four-legged animal.

- Using a butcher's knife and saw, separate the hock from one of the haunches (pic 1, p.166). The hock can then be used for braising and the haunch tied for roasting on the bone. Here, the other haunch will be turned into steaks.

- Take the small fillets and kidneys from the inside of the saddle. Now split the saddle in two by cutting with the knife and saw through the spine at the point level with the backmost ribs (pic 2). This makes a great little roasting joint.

- The meat can be cut from the remaining saddle to create loins or cannons (pic 3). Keep the bones for stock and any meat trimmings for use in stews, or for mincing to make burgers, sausages etc.

- The rib bones can be French trimmed, then chined. To chine, make a cut along the spine down to the ribs with the knife, thus freeing up the meat so it won't get damaged as you use the cleaver to chop through the rib bones with the saddle standing on end. The chined, trimmed loin can then either be cut between each rib bone into individual cutlets or cut into larger racks (pic 4).

- If you decide to make boneless loins for steaks or roasting, remove the silver skin from the loin by working the tip of the knife under it, then running the knife along the loin while holding the end of the sinew strip (pic 5). Repeat until all the skin is removed. Tie the loin for roasting or cut into steaks.

- Take the second haunch and begin to separate the muscles by cutting between them (pic 6). This is known as 'seaming out' and results in lots of smaller steak-quality chunks of meat, as each muscle will be far more tender if cooked separately after removal of the silver skin and sinews. Take your time here: use your fingers to explore where the muscle edges go and assess how best to separate them. You want to avoid cutting into the muscles.

- Trim any remnants of meat from the haunch bone (pic 7) and set them aside for mincing or stewing. Remove the hock and put it with the other one; keep the bone for stock.

- Finally, either cut the seamed-out haunch meat into steaks (pic 8) or tie it for roasting as small joints. Give everything a final check over and trim if needed.

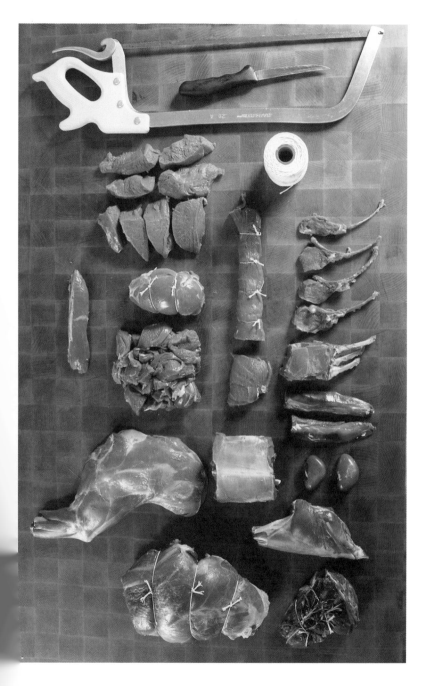

Further butchering a deer

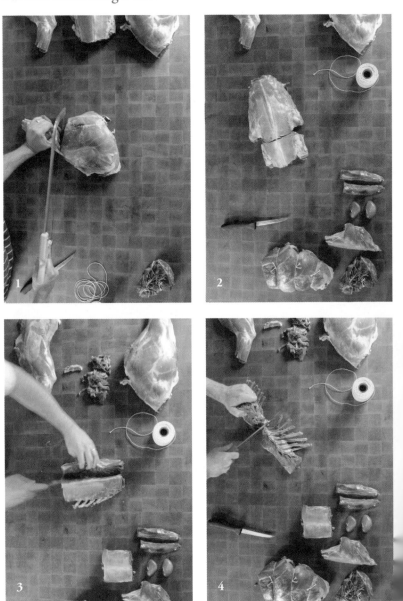

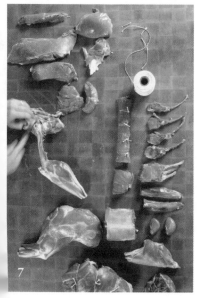

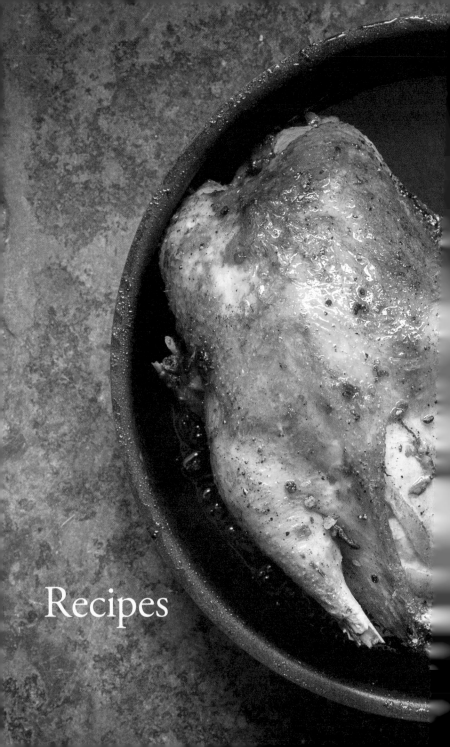

Recipes

Roasted hen pheasant

Every now and again, when you get hold of some very good hen birds early in the season, a traditional roast is the only way to go. A young pheasant is like the ultimate guinea fowl, with a little more texture and a lot more flavour. As a Sunday roast goes, with crunchy fried game chips, bread sauce and lashings of homemade gravy, it's one of the best. Serve with whatever veggies you fancy – the Cover crop crumble on p.173 would be the perfect choice.

Serves 2

1 oven-ready hen pheasant
A little pork fat or goose/duck fat
A few sage leaves
Sea salt and freshly ground
    black pepper

For the bread sauce
A good knob of butter
½ onion, peeled and finely chopped
150ml whole milk
50–100g day-old bread, crusts
    removed, cubed
A little freshly grated nutmeg

For the gravy
A glass of dry cider
1 litre dark game stock (see p.207),
    or chicken stock will do

For the game chips
200g potatoes, peeled, washed
    and dried
300ml sunflower or vegetable oil,
    for deep-frying
A pinch of paprika

Take your bird out of the fridge an hour or so before cooking, to bring it to room temperature.

Preheat the oven to 200°C/Gas mark 6. Rub a little fat over the bird and season it generously, inside and out. Place a few sage leaves inside the cavity and under the breast skin. Don't be tempted to tie the bird up: this impedes the cooking of the legs and is likely to result in overcooking of the breast meat.

Place a heavy-based ovenproof frying pan over a medium-high heat. When it is hot, add a little fat. Once melted, lay the bird on its back in the pan and cook for around 5 minutes until coloured. Turn and brown each side of the bird in the same way, then return it to its back.

Transfer the pan to the oven for about 15 minutes to finish the cooking – the breasts should be firmed up nicely. Then leave the bird, uncovered, in a warm place to rest for about half an hour.

Meanwhile, to make the bread sauce, melt the butter in a medium saucepan over a medium-low heat. Add the chopped onion and sweat for 4–5 minutes until slightly translucent. Season well with salt and pepper and add the milk. Bring to a simmer and stir in the bread; the sauce will be thin at this stage. Add a little grated nutmeg but don't overdo it (the flavour will intensify as the sauce rests). Set aside in a warm spot to rest and thicken.

To make the gravy, boil the cider in a pan until it has reduced down to a quarter of its original volume, then add the stock. Continue to reduce down until slightly thickened and rich-tasting.

To make the game chips, thinly slice your potatoes (using a mandoline, if you have one) and drain well on kitchen paper. Heat your oil in a deep, heavy-based pan to 180°C (or until a piece of bread dropped into the oil turns golden brown in 1 minute). Deep-fry the potato slices, in batches, for about 3–5 minutes until crisp. Transfer them to kitchen paper to drain, then season with salt, pepper and paprika; keep hot.

To finish the gravy, add the roasting juices from the pheasant pan, stir well and pass through a sieve into a warm jug.

To serve, carve slices of the breast and joint the legs in the same way as you would a roast chicken. Serve with the hot gravy, game chips, bread sauce and veggies of your choice.

Cover crop crumble

I have, on occasion, cooked for people who have an aversion to vegetables. I was cooking roast venison for some friendly folk in Lancashire and placed a big bowl of buttered blanched kale on the table. My host, who is not renowned for his subtlety, looked me straight in the eye and said, 'Around here, kale is something pheasants hide in, not something you eat.' I took this as a challenge – to come up with a kale dish that would pass muster at a veg-dodgers' table. This combination of greens, cream and crunch is the result. It is great with any game, especially Roasted hen pheasant (p.171). You can vary the greens if you wish.

Serves 2

4 good handfuls of kale, washed
A good knob of butter
1 onion, peeled and finely chopped
½ glass of white wine
1 tbsp plain white flour
300ml double cream
2 garlic cloves, peeled and
    finely chopped
Sea salt and freshly ground
    black pepper

For the crumble topping
100g day-old good white bread
2 garlic cloves, peeled and roughly
    chopped
A good sprig of parsley, roughly
    chopped
A little olive oil, to drizzle

Preheat the oven to 180°C/Gas mark 4. Strip the stalks from the kale leaves and chop them finely. Chop the leaves according to their texture, i.e. thinly at their thicker base and more thickly towards the top; set both stalks and leaves aside.

Heat the butter in a pan over a fairly low heat and add the onion and chopped kale stalks. Sweat for about 10 minutes until tender. Add the kale leaves, followed by the wine and cook until the kale has wilted and the wine has lost its sour edge – around 5 minutes or so. Stir in the flour, then the cream and garlic and simmer for a minute or two until the sauce thickens. Season well with salt and pepper to taste.

For the topping, blitz the bread with the garlic and parsley in a food processor to fine crumbs.

Transfer the kale mixture to an ovenproof dish, about 20cm square and 5cm deep. Cover with the breadcrumb mixture and drizzle with olive oil. Cook in the oven for about 15 minutes until golden and bubbling. This veg dish is so good that I often eat it on its own, or with cold roast game torn over the top.

Game ragu

This is one of those dishes that is less of a faff than it might seem. It takes a while to cook, but for most of that time you can just ignore it and let it do its own thing. Timewise, it will more than pay you back when you need a quick lunch dish at the drop of a hat as, once the batch is done, you can freeze it in portion sizes that suit your needs. It makes a great sauce for pasta, a good base for stews or, with the addition of a few lentils and a little more stock, it can be served as a hearty soup. I have given quantities for 10 portions, but you can easily scale it up or down according to how much pheasant leg you have to hand. I also do the same dish with rabbit, hare, wild boar and grey squirrel (you'll need 5 squirrels).

Serves 10

500ml game stock, light or dark (see p.207), or chicken stock will do
A handful of dried ceps
2 onions, peeled
1 large carrot, peeled
1 celery stick
4 garlic cloves, peeled
Rapeseed or light olive oil, for cooking
10 pheasant legs on the bone, thighs separated from drumsticks

2 rashers of streaky bacon (smoked or unsmoked), chopped
1 tsp coriander seeds
½ cinnamon stick
1 tsp each chopped thyme and rosemary, or a good pinch of dried mixed herbs
500ml tomato passata
A glass of dry cider
Sea salt and freshly ground black pepper

Preheat the oven to 120°C/Gas mark ½.

Heat your stock in a pan to simmering point, then remove from the heat and drop in the dried ceps. Leave for about 15 minutes until they are tender, then fish them out and chop them finely. Strain the stock through a muslin-lined sieve or coffee filter paper to get rid of any grit; set aside.

Finely chop the onions, carrot, celery and garlic. You can do all this in a blender if you like, pulsing the veg until well chopped.

Place a large flameproof casserole dish over a medium-high heat and add a little oil. Season the pheasant legs generously with salt and pepper and brown them in the hot pan, in batches, transferring the pheasant to a plate once it is coloured.

When all the pheasant is browned, add the bacon to the pan, followed by the chopped ceps, vegetables, garlic, spices and herbs. Lower the heat and cook for around 10 minutes, to soften the vegetables. Add the passata and cook for another 10 minutes, adjusting the seasoning as you go.

Now add the cider and stock and bring to a slow simmer. Add the browned pheasant, put the lid on and put in the oven for 4 hours. Take it out of the oven to check if the meat is tender; it should be just about falling off the bone by this point. If, however, it's still a little tough when you taste it, put it back in the oven and leave it for another hour.

Once it is cooked, leave to cool and then lift out the pheasant legs from the sauce. Pick out the bones and sinews and return the meat to the sauce. Stir well and check the seasoning. The ragu is now ready to serve, or you can keep it in the fridge or freezer for later use.

If serving the ragu with pasta, toss through and finish with a scattering of chopped parsley, freshly grated Parmesan and a trickle of extra virgin olive oil, if you like.

Lasagne of game
and wild mushrooms

One of the great things about late autumn is that you get a nice crossover between the pheasant shooting season and the wild mushroom harvest. It will vary slightly from area to area and depend highly on the prevailing weather conditions, but, with luck, you should be able to get hold of some winter chanterelles and a few early-season cock pheasants at the same time. You can, of course, use hen pheasants instead, but I usually save those tender birds for roasting (see p.171).

Mallard, pigeon, partridge and venison also work very well in this recipe.

Serves 4–6

For the ragu
2 pheasant thighs and 2 breasts
50g rindless smoked bacon
Good olive oil, for cooking
1 onion, peeled and finely diced
2 garlic cloves, peeled and chopped
A good sprig of rosemary, leaves only, finely chopped
A couple of sprigs of thyme, leaves only, finely chopped
A pinch of dried chilli flakes
½ tsp caraway seeds
A glass of red wine
400g tin good-quality peeled plum tomatoes, pushed through a sieve
500ml light game stock (p.207)
350g chanterelles, or other wild mushrooms (chestnut mushrooms will do at a push)
Sea salt and freshly ground black pepper

For the pasta
200g white spelt flour, or '00' pasta flour
1 whole egg, plus about 3 egg yolks

For the white sauce
20g butter
15g plain white flour
500ml light game stock (p.207)
250ml double cream

To finish
250g good strong hard cheese, such as a mature Cheddar

Equipment
Mincer

Remove the skin from the pheasant and the bones from the legs (see pp.150–3). Put all the pheasant meat and bacon through a mincer fitted with a medium blade.

In a large pan over a medium-high heat, heat a splash of olive oil, then fry the minced pheasant meat and bacon in small batches until just a little brown and no

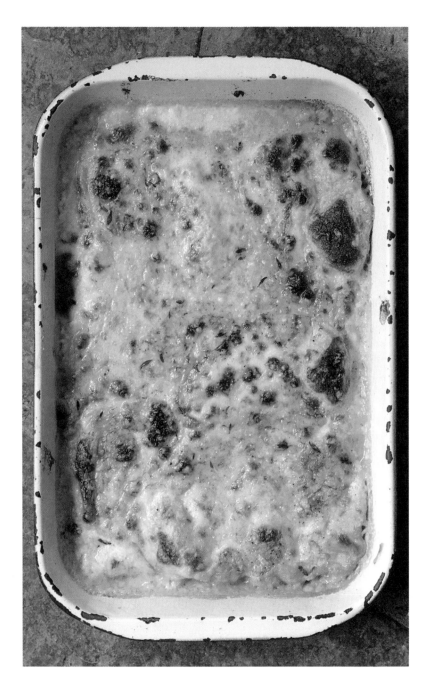

longer raw-looking. This will take around 6–8 minutes: don't overload the pan or you will end up stewing the meat. Once it's all coloured, return all the meat to the pan and add the onion, garlic, rosemary, thyme, chilli flakes and caraway seeds and cook, stirring occasionally, for 10–15 minutes.

Add the wine and cook for a few minutes to reduce, then add the sieved tomatoes and cook for another 15 minutes. Now add the stock, season with salt and pepper and simmer for an hour or so until the sauce is nicely rich and tasty.

While the sauce is simmering away, clean and prepare your mushrooms: break them in half by pulling the trumpet end apart to ensure there are no pine needles hidden in the tubular stem. Heat a splash of oil in a frying pan and fry the mushrooms quickly, seasoning them with salt and pepper, until just starting to wilt. Transfer to a plate to cool.

To make the pasta, work the flour, whole egg and two of the egg yolks together to make a smooth, firm, pliable dough, adding the third yolk if needed; this should only take 5 minutes or so. The texture should be soft enough to manipulate without making your arms ache, but tough and elastic enough to tolerate rolling without the addition of too much extra flour as you go. If you don't have a pasta machine, then you may need to add a little more water to make it easier to roll by hand. Wrap the pasta dough in lightly oiled cling film and rest in the fridge for at least 5 minutes.

To make the white sauce, melt the butter in a saucepan and mix in the flour to make a smooth roux. Cook, stirring, over a fairly low heat, for a minute or so, then slowly add the stock, a little at a time, beating well to make a smooth, thick sauce. (Unlike most flour-based sauces, you don't need to cook the floury taste out of the sauce at this stage, as it will have plenty of time in the oven later.) Add the cream and season well.

Preheat the oven to 190°C/Gas mark 5. Roll your pasta into thin sheets using a pasta machine or a rolling pin. Make sure it is thin enough that you can just see through it – about the thickness of 3 sheets of copier paper or the front cover of a glossy magazine. Layer it up between sheets of floured greaseproof paper so it doesn't stick together again.

Layer everything in a fairly deep baking dish, about 20 x 30cm, starting with some white sauce and mushrooms, followed by some of the ragu, then a layer of pasta. Repeat these layers to use all the ingredients, finishing with a layer of mushrooms topped with white sauce. Grate the cheese over this top layer. Bake in the oven for about 30–40 minutes until golden and bubbling. Remove from the oven and allow to stand for 10 minutes before serving.

Partridge with pumpkin
and cider

This is a simple supper for a big party, or indeed a small one – as the leftovers are excellent cold or reheated. Partridge and pumpkin are ideal seasonal bedfellows and their exchange of flavours in this recipe is underpinned wonderfully by the acidic sweetness of the cider. Although the dish is moist, it's not a stew; it's a kind of steam-roasted affair that makes the most of the ingredients with minimum effort. Make sure you choose a variety of pumpkin (or squash) that's tasty and not just ornamental. I like Turk's Turban or Hundredweight.

Serves 6

6 oven-ready partridges
A knob of butter
1kg good, firm pumpkin flesh,
    i.e. 1 peeled and deseeded small
    pumpkin, or chunk of a large one
A handful of sage leaves
A few bay leaves

2 tsp coriander seeds
Rapeseed oil, to drizzle
300ml good dry cider
250ml dark game stock (p.207)
Sea salt and freshly ground
    black pepper

Preheat the oven to 200°C/Gas mark 6.

Select a robust roasting tin large enough to hold all the ingredients comfortably. If the partridges will be touching and half buried by the pumpkin it will be too crowded, so you'll need to use 2 roasting tins (or one larger one).

Season your partridges and rub them with a knob of butter. Place them in the roasting tin breast side up. Cut the pumpkin into generous chunks and distribute around the birds. Scatter over the sage, bay leaves and coriander seeds and drizzle liberally with rapeseed oil.

Roast in the hot oven for 15 minutes until the partridges are browned then turn the oven down to 160°C/Gas mark 3. Add the cider and stock and cook for a further 10 minutes or so before removing from the oven. Set aside to rest in a warm place for 10 minutes.

This is best served in a help-yourself fashion – plonk it on the table, put out some bread to go with it and let everyone tuck in.

Old grouse noodle soup

Young grouse are tender and very tasty without being overpowering, and I would recommend roasting them whole (see p.59). Old grouse, however, are far stronger in flavour and simply roasting them whole isn't really an option. Their depth of flavour needs a fairly hefty counterbalance, which soy, ginger and chilli supply here. Egg noodles add body to this lovely light, tasty broth, which I like to finish with a scattering of greens. The recipe also works well with older mallard.

Serves 4 as a starter, or 2 as a main dish

2 oven-ready old grouse
About 2 litres water
5 garlic cloves, peeled
100ml dark soy sauce
5cm piece of fresh root ginger, sliced
    into fine discs, about 3mm thick
1 star anise
2 hot red chillies
A little rapeseed oil, for cooking

¼ tsp Chinese five-spice powder
200g dried egg noodles
Sea salt and freshly ground
    black pepper

To serve
Sliced spring onions
Shredded green cabbage
Snipped chives

Preheat the oven to 180°C/Gas mark 4.

Remove the breasts from the grouse by cutting along the side of the breastbone and set them aside for use later on. Place the grouse legs and carcasses in a suitable ovenproof dish and roast in the oven for 20 minutes until nicely coloured.

Put the legs and carcasses into a deep saucepan and pour on enough water to cover. Slowly bring to a simmer and skim off any scum that forms on the surface. Add the whole garlic cloves and soy sauce along with the ginger, star anise and a whole red chilli. Cook at a gentle simmer for 1 hour. Remove from the heat and allow to cool a little before passing through a sieve. Discard the carcasses and legs.

Place a large frying pan over a medium-high heat and add a little rapeseed oil. Season the grouse breasts liberally with salt, pepper and five-spice powder. Add them to the hot pan and cook for 2–3 minutes on each side. Remove from the pan and leave to rest on a warm plate.

Meanwhile, bring 1 litre of the flavoured stock to the boil. Add the noodles, return to a simmer and cook until just tender. Slice the grouse breasts and divide among warmed serving bowls. Ladle over the hot stock and noodles and add the spring onions, shredded cabbage, finely sliced remaining chilli and chives.

Roasted woodcock or snipe

Seriously tasty little birds, woodcock and snipe are rare treats. As and when you do get hold of a few, there is no better way to serve them than simply roasted, with their lightly cooked innards spread on some good toast. You need to roast them in a pan and then in the oven, using intense heat that will fill the kitchen with smoke, but with these little birds it's the only way. You must roast them hard (but briefly) to get a good release of flavour without drying them out.

Serves 2

2 woodcock or 4 snipe, plucked, wings
   and heads removed, guts left in
A knob of butter
1 garlic clove, peeled and very
   finely chopped
A few thyme leaves
Sea salt and freshly ground
   black pepper

To serve
Some decent toast
Crab apple (or other fruit) jelly
   (optional)

Preheat the oven to 220°C/Gas mark 7. Place a large heavy-based ovenproof frying pan over a high heat to get it nice and hot. Season your birds with salt and pepper. Add a little butter to the hot pan, then add the birds, placing them on their backs. Roast in the pan, without moving, for about 2–3 minutes until the backs are golden. Now turn them first on to one side, then the other, to colour in the same way. Then flip the birds over, add a little more butter and colour the breasts a little.

Turn the birds over on to their backs again and put the pan in the hot oven. Roast for a few minutes until the guts just begin to pop out of the birds, then remove the pan from the oven (remember to use an oven glove to grab the handle). Transfer the birds from the pan to a warm plate to rest for a few minutes.

Place the pan over a low heat and get ready with a fork and the garlic. Use the fork to scoop out the innards of the birds (from their back end) into the pan. Add the garlic and thyme leaves, then mash the innards up with the back of the fork and cook for just a minute or so. Remove from the heat before they dry out.

Quickly spread the cooked guts on hot toast. Place a piece of toast and one bird (two for snipe) on each warmed plate and serve. Use your fingers to eat them, nibbling off the little bits of flesh that get left on the carcass. You don't really need any accompaniment, but something sweet like a crab apple jelly would work well.

Pigeon with blackberries
and chanterelles

This is as seasonal as food gets. In late summer, when the grains are being harvested, pigeons take the opportunity to help themselves to whatever the combine harvester leaves behind. At the same time, chanterelles are popping up in the woods and the hedgerows are groaning with blackberries. Lunch is looking good. This recipe also works well with duck breasts.

Serves 2

Rapeseed oil, for cooking
4 plump pigeon breasts (easily removed, see pp.150–3)
2 good handfuls of chanterelles, trimmed and brushed clean of grit

A knob of butter
A good handful of blackberries
A couple of handfuls of salad leaves
Sea salt and freshly ground black pepper

Place a heavy-based frying pan over a high heat and add a little rapeseed oil. Season the pigeon breasts with salt and pepper and add them to the hot pan. Give them a minute or two, until they start to form a nice caramelised layer on the base. Now turn them over and add the chanterelles and butter at the same time. After about another 2 minutes, once the pigeon breasts are firm but not overcooked, remove them to a warm plate and set aside in a warm spot to rest.

Finish cooking the chanterelles for another minute or two, then lift them out and put them with the pigeon.

Turn off the heat and pop the blackberries into the pan to warm and release a little juice. Add any resting juices from the pigeon and mushrooms to the berries.

Divide the salad leaves between a couple of plates. Slice the pigeon breasts and arrange on the leaves, then scatter over the mushrooms. Spoon on the blackberries and sprinkle over the juices from the pan. Drizzle with a little more rapeseed oil if you think it needs it and serve with some fresh crusty bread.

Pigeon and bacon burgers

This recipe is so simple, it should be a standard for all burgers. It works particularly well with pigeon as the sweet smokiness of the bacon offsets the richness of the iron-y red pigeon meat very well indeed, but it is almost as good with wild duck breasts or venison.

Serves 4

250g boneless pigeon breast meat,
  skin removed
250g dry-cured smoked streaky bacon,
  rind removed
A good knob of butter
A few bay leaves
Freshly ground black pepper

To serve
4 bread rolls or slices of toast, spread
  with dripping or butter
Mustard, ketchup and/or other
  embellishments of your choice

Equipment
Mincer

Roughly cut the pigeon and bacon into chunks. Fit your mincer with the coarse blade. Mince the meats together, then mix well by hand and pass the mixture through the mincer again.

Divide the mixture into 4 even portions. Form these into thick burgers using your hands, or a burger press if you have one. Place the burgers in the fridge to firm up for an hour or two before cooking.

Heat a large non-stick frying pan over a medium-high heat (or you can cook the burgers on a barbecue or under a hot grill if you prefer). Season the burgers with a little pepper (you won't need salt as the bacon will provide enough). When the pan is really hot, add the burgers and sear on one side without moving for around 5 minutes; if things start to get a bit smoky, turn down the heat slightly. Don't be tempted to faff about with the burgers; leave them alone as prodding and poking can cause them to fall apart or release precious moisture.

Once the burgers are well browned on the underside, turn them over in the pan, add the butter and bay leaves and cook for a further 5 minutes. Then turn off the heat and leave the burgers in the pan to rest for 5 minutes.

Serve the burgers in bread rolls or on dripping (or buttered) toast, with whatever embellishments you like.

P.S. I like these burgers slightly pink; if you don't, then cook them a little longer.

Game Caesar salad

Caesar salad is an American invention – crunchy romaine lettuce, a rich garlic and anchovy dressing and crunchy croûtons marrying with Parmesan to great effect. Chicken is often added too but in my adaptation I'm using rook, which gives the salad a greater depth of flavour, and Cheddar rather than Parmesan. It also works well with pigeon, wigeon, mallard, partridge and pheasant.

Serves 2

1 little gem or ½ romaine lettuce
¼ day-old baguette
Light olive oil, for cooking
4 young rook (or other game) breasts
A good chunk of very mature
    Cheddar cheese (about 60g)
Sea salt and freshly ground
    black pepper

For the dressing
1 egg yolk
1 garlic clove, peeled and finely
    chopped
Juice of 1 lemon
1 tsp French mustard
4 anchovy fillets, chopped
About 100ml light olive oil

Preheat the oven to 180°C/Gas mark 4. Wash your lettuce and drain it well. Spin in a salad spinner if you have one or leave to drain thoroughly in a colander. If the lettuce is too wet it will dilute the dressing and ruin the dish.

Slice the baguette into 5mm thick rounds and lay them out on a baking sheet. Drizzle with a little olive oil and season well with salt and pepper. Bake in the oven until golden and crunchy, about 10 minutes.

To make the dressing, beat the egg yolk, chopped garlic, lemon juice, mustard and chopped anchovies together in a bowl. Then slowly drizzle in enough olive oil, whisking all the time, to thicken the dressing slightly and balance the acidity of the lemon juice. Season well with pepper.

Place a heavy-based frying pan over a high heat. When hot, add a little olive oil, followed by the rook breasts. Pan-roast for around 2 minutes on each side, then remove from the heat and leave the rook breasts to rest in the hot pan for about 5 minutes. Make sure you leave them slightly pink or they will taste a little liver-y.

To assemble your salad, arrange the lettuce leaves in a salad bowl and finely grate half of the cheese over the lettuce. Roughly tear the croûtes into the salad and drizzle generously with the dressing. Cut the rook breasts into slices and arrange on the salad. Using a vegetable peeler, shave over the rest of the cheese and trickle over a little more dressing; serve the rest separately (you may not need all of it).

Slow-roast spiced soy duck

This is my version of the classic Chinese takeaway, using wild duck instead of farmed. This works very well indeed as the depth of flavour in wild duck stands up to the spices and salty sweetness of the sauce. Be careful when you make it, as it can lead to a compulsion to make it again and again. The recipe also works well with pink-footed goose, and with pheasant – if you baste it with duck fat during roasting to keep it moist.

Serves 4–6

1 lemongrass stem
2 oven-ready wild ducks (mallard, wigeon etc.)
1 litre water
About 1 tsp sesame oil
About 1 tbsp tomato passata or ketchup
A little soy sauce and/or honey, to season (optional)

For the spice paste
1 tsp coriander seeds
1 tsp fennel seeds
½ star anise
1 tsp Chinese five-spice powder

4 tbsp good soy sauce (rich and thick)
2 tbsp honey
2–3cm piece of fresh root ginger, fairly finely chopped
½ tsp dried chilli flakes

To serve
Chinese-style pancakes or flour tortillas (see p.195, made with sesame rather than vegetable oil)
Sliced spring onion
Cucumber sticks
Coriander leaves

Preheat the oven to 180°C/Gas mark 4. Bash the lemongrass to release the flavour – lightly for a subtle hint, or heavily for a stronger flavour. Place in a deep roasting dish and sit the ducks on top.

For the spice paste, toast the coriander and fennel seeds and the star anise briefly in a hot, dry pan to release their fragrance, then crush using a pestle and mortar. Combine the crushed spices with the five-spice powder, soy, honey, ginger and chilli flakes. Smear this mixture all over the ducks. (You can do this the day before cooking to achieve a really deep flavour, but simply spreading it on just before cooking gives a perfectly satisfactory result.) Pour the water into the roasting dish, around but not over the ducks, and place the whole show in the oven.

Now, once it's all in the oven, it will require a little nurturing. After about half an hour, baste the ducks with the liquid in the tray and turn the oven down to

140°C/Gas mark 1. Repeat the basting every 30 or 40 minutes until the ducks are tender: about 2 or 3 hours will do it. The more often you baste them, the better they will be. Baste more often towards the end of the cooking time. You will find the liquor in the tray reduces and intensifies, but if it starts to dry out completely, add a little more water – or the ingredients will burn and the whole shebang will be as bitter as dandelion tea.

Once the ducks are done, and the meat is just starting to fall off the bone, transfer them to a warm dish and set aside to rest in a warm place while you make the sauce and get the garnishes ready. (You can, at this stage, let them cool completely, and reheat them later in a hot oven.)

Stir the sesame oil and tomato passata into the leftover juices in the roasting dish to achieve a loose, barbecue sauce consistency. Taste and adjust the seasoning, adding extra soy if it needs more salt, and/or honey if it needs a little sweetening.

To serve, take the duck meat off the bone and shred it. I normally just pull the meat off in a rough and ready way, using a pair of tongs and a fork. Serve alongside little pancakes or tortillas, bowls of sliced spring onion, cucumber sticks and coriander leaves, and the lovely savoury sauce.

Spicy fajitas

This is an excellent way to introduce game to people who are reluctant to try it. All you need is a frying pan, a handful of storecupboard ingredients and a source of heat and you're away. You can, of course, make it more or less of a feast by adding extras to the final assembly, such as coriander chutney, hot sauce or guacamole, but a simple version with just a little natural yoghurt is just as good.

I'm also hoping that this simple recipe will introduce you to the wonders of homemade flour tortillas. Those you buy ready-made are sad little substitutes for the real thing.

You can use rabbit, wild boar, pheasant or muntjac for the fajitas, but I think they work best with wild duck.

Serves 4

For the tortillas

200g plain white flour or white spelt flour, with a little sifted wholemeal added if you like

A good pinch of salt

A good glug of sunflower oil, or light olive oil

About 100ml tap-cold water

For the filling

4 mallard (or other duck) breasts, skin removed

½ onion, peeled

2 garlic cloves, peeled

1 tsp coriander seeds

1 tsp cumin seeds

1 tsp caraway seeds

½ tsp fennel seeds

2 tsp smoked paprika

A good glug of rapeseed or light olive oil

Sea salt and freshly ground black pepper

To serve

Natural yoghurt

Mint and coriander leaves

To make the tortillas, combine all the ingredients in a bowl and work together briefly to form a smooth dough that is soft, elastic and pliable but not in any way sticky. You are trying for the perfect balance between moisture and rollability. Then put the dough on a lightly floured surface, turn the bowl upside down and place it over the dough to keep the air out and let it rest for 5 minutes or so.

Tear off pieces of dough the size of small plums and roll into balls. Roll these out with a rolling pin until as thin as you can handle without breaking. Heat a dry frying pan over a moderate heat. Pop one of the rolled-out tortillas in the hot frying pan and cook briefly, about 45 seconds on each side: they should puff up

nicely and acquire a dappling of brown spots. Don't cook them too slowly or they will dry out and refuse to play ball later on. Cook them over too high a heat and they will burn and be raw at the same time.

As they cook, place them in a pile on a plate, covering them with a tea towel to keep them warm and soft. They will keep warm for around 20 minutes, but if they are cold when you come to use them you can reheat them briefly in the oven or give the whole lot 20 seconds in the microwave.

Cut the duck breasts into slices, the thickness of a £1 coin, and place them in a bowl. Thinly slice the onion and garlic and add them to the bowl.

Heat a dry frying pan over a medium heat. Add all the spice seeds and toast briefly to wake them up a bit. Tip them into a mortar and roughly grind with the pestle, leaving some character in the spice mix.

Add the spice mix, along with the paprika and a little salt and pepper, to the meat and onion. Add a glug of rapeseed or olive oil and mix gently. Leave to marinate for a few minutes. (You can marinate it overnight if you wish but you will need to leave out the salt or the meat will cure.)

Turn the heat up under the frying pan and, once it's good and hot, add your marinated meat and onion. Avoid stirring it immediately, as you want a little colour on the meat, and some charred onion is a good thing in the right place. After a minute or so, turn the meat, then leave it alone again for about 1–2 minutes. Stir again and turn off the heat, but leave in the pan to finish cooking and to rest for around 5 minutes. You want the meat a tiny bit pink and certainly not dry.

To serve, I like to place the meat, tortillas, yoghurt and herbs on the table and allow people to dive in and help themselves. Start with a warm tortilla, add a good spoonful of the meat mixture, then spoon on a little yoghurt, sprinkle in a couple of mint leaves and some fresh coriander, wrap it all up and eat nonchalantly. It's an off-the-cuff kind of dish and you should tune your attitude to match.

P.S. I use white spelt flour for just about everything in the kitchen. It's strong enough for pasta, bread, tortillas and pizza, yet just about soft enough for pastry and cakes. It's up to you of course what you use, but a bag of white spelt means you have fewer packets of flour to fumble around with, looking for the right one.

Duck 'bacon' and eggs

This is a favourite breakfast of mine in the winter, when the day's activities call for a little more than tea and toast to sustain body and soul until lunchtime. It's also a good opportunity to introduce yourself to a spot of simple curing. Curing in its most basic form is the removal of water from meat via the process of osmosis, by applying salt and sugar to the meat. Pigeon breasts can be treated in the same way.

Serves 4

4 mallard breasts, with or without skin

For the quick cure

2 peppercorns
1 point from a star anise
1 bay leaf
2 tsp table salt
2 tsp light brown sugar

To serve
4 generous slices of good bread
A little oil or butter
4 eggs

To prepare the cure, crush the peppercorns and star anise, finely chop the bay leaf and mix these with the salt and sugar.

Season the duck breasts generously with the cure, sprinkling it over both sides (you may not need it all). Place them in a ceramic, plastic or non-reactive metal container in the fridge for at least 2 hours, but no longer than 4 hours. They should give up some liquid and become a little firmer but the object here is not to cure them all the way through: you want duck 'bacon' on the outside but fresh duck on the inside. Rinse off the cure and pat the breasts dry.

Place the meat in a clean dish and leave in the fridge, uncovered, for an hour or two to dry slightly, before covering. The breasts are now ready to use, but will be better in a day or two when the meat will have developed in flavour and character.

To prepare your duck 'bacon' breakfast, slice the duck breasts thinly lengthways into 'rashers'. Heat a frying pan and put some bread in the toaster. Add a little butter or oil to the pan and fry your rashers of duck until just cooked. Remove them from the pan and keep them warm while you fry the eggs in the same pan. Serve with the toast and enjoy.

Quick-smoked duck

Quick-smoking imparts a smoky, salty sweetness and gentle spicing, lending a sophisticated flavour to duck flesh. The process also prolongs the life of the meat and makes it more suitable for freezing. Once smoked, the breasts still need to be cooked before eating, but you can cook them pink, or however you like them. Pop a few of these beauties in the freezer and you'll never be far from a quick and easy supper, lunch or canapé. Pigeon, pheasant and partridge breasts are also suitable.

Makes 6 smoked duck breasts (to serve 4)

6 mallard (or other duck) breasts

For the quick cure
2 peppercorns, roughly crushed
1 bay leaf, shredded
1 point from a star anise, crushed
2 tsp light brown sugar
2 tsp table salt

Equipment
Smoker (see below)
Wood shavings

Mix all the cure ingredients together. Put the duck breasts in a ceramic dish or plastic tub, add the cure and rub it liberally over the meat. Leave to cure for about 15 minutes, until it has given off a little moisture and firmed up slightly.

Rinse off the cure under cold running water and pat the duck breasts dry using a clean tea towel.

Now, set up your smoker and get the smoke going. Pop the breasts inside and smoke for 3–5 minutes, depending on how hot your smoker is. Do not fully cook them – you only want to offer them a hint of smoky flavour.

Once out of the smoker, you can cook the duck breasts in a pan with a little duck fat or butter to medium, and they will be seriously tasty, either eaten straight away or allowed to cool and then sliced. Alternatively, you can freeze them without cooking. They can also be kept in the fridge for up to a week before cooking.

To make a hot smoker

You will need two baking trays of the same size with a wire rack between them. The wood shavings go in the bottom tray, the rack is loaded with the meat and the top tray sits over them to trap the smoke. The whole thing is then placed on the heat to get the wood shavings smoking. Simple off-the-shelf versions are available from kitchen stores, fishing tackle shops and online.

Goose sausages

Goose… big, tough goose. If you have a glut of goose meat, turning it into sausages is a good solution. You can make them yourself if you have a mincer and a sausage stuffer – or you could get a friendly butcher to do it for you. Either way, a packet of goose and pork sausages is a great thing to have in the fridge or freezer.

Chipolata-style sheep's runners are the best skins to use for these sausages. You can get these processed, salted sheep's intestines from online suppliers, or a good butcher. Or, if you can't be doing with filling sausage skins, opt for burgers.

Remove the goose meat from the bone as for a pheasant (see pp.150–3). The skin is tougher, so you'll find it quite tricky. Persevere – it's worth it.

Cook your sausages (or burgers) in the usual way.

Makes around 24 chipolatas

1kg wild goose meat (any species),
  off the bone
250g very fatty pork belly
10g salt
5g dried mixed herbs
1 tsp fennel seeds, lightly toasted
  and crushed
15 white peppercorns, crushed

3g ground black pepper
100g fine breadcrumbs (optional)
About 3 metres sheep's runners,
  soaked in cold water overnight

Equipment
Mincer
Sausage stuffer

Pass the goose and pork through the medium plate of the mincer into a large bowl, then add the salt, herbs and spices. If you want to use breadcrumbs, add those too. Put the seasoned mix back through the mincer again to take the texture down a little more and mix everything really well.

Now fill the sausage casings as you would for any other sausage: put the seasoned sausage mix into the sausage stuffer and load the runners on to the spout, using cold water to help them slide on and off the spout. Then, applying pressure to the piston end of the sausage stuffer with the handle, fill the cases. Adjusting the firmness of the grip you have on the sausage skins will alter their thickness.

Once you've made them into one long sausage, twist them into the desired lengths and link them up so they don't unravel, either using a traditional butcher's link or simply by tying a small knot of string between each. Let them hang up to dry a little in the fridge for a day or so before cutting into individual sausages and, if necessary, freezing for later use. Make sure you tie off the ends or you may come back later to discover all the filling has dropped out of your carefully crafted snags!

Gamekeeper's pie

Easy and satisfying, this cottage pie made with game is winter comfort food at its best. I've added a little rooty flourish to the topping to set off the rich game. If you don't have potatoes and celeriac, top the filling with a simple pastry lid, or thick bread slices smothered in garlic butter and bake in the same way. Buttered greens on the side are a must.

You can use pretty much any game meat for this pie. Goose breasts work well and shoulder of venison is great, or you can use pheasant or wild duck, or any combination of these.

Serves 5–6

2 onions, peeled
1 carrot, peeled
1 celery stick
A little rapeseed oil
500g minced game (whatever you have, see above)
100g minced pork belly (as fatty as possible)
3 garlic cloves, peeled and finely chopped
A glass of red wine
400g tin good-quality peeled plum tomatoes, pushed through a sieve
A sprig each of thyme and rosemary, finely chopped

1 litre game stock (see p.207), or any other meat stock
A good pinch of ground mace
1 star anise
Sea salt and freshly ground black pepper

For the topping
450g peeled celeriac
600ml whole milk
750g floury potatoes, such as King Edwards, peeled
100g butter, melted
1 egg yolk

Finely dice the veg, either by hand or in a food processor. Heat a little oil in a large flameproof casserole over a fairly high heat. Add the minced meat and allow to colour, stirring as necessary. Once the meat is browning nicely, start adding the chopped veg and garlic, maintaining a good steady sizzle.

Once all the meat has coloured up nicely and the veg is beginning to soften, add the wine and allow to simmer and reduce for a few minutes to lose its acidity; if you can smell a sour acidity in the steam coming off the pan, leave it to simmer a little longer. Then add the sieved tomatoes and chopped herbs and cook for 5 minutes or so, to intensify and sweeten the mixture.

Pour in the stock, add the mace and star anise and bring to a simmer.

Put a lid on the pan and cook over a very low heat, so it's just simmering, for around 2 hours, adding a little water if it seems to be getting too dry. Once nicely thickened and tender, season well, and leave to rest. (You could finish this process in a low oven at around 150°C/Gas mark 2 if you prefer; that way you don't need to keep as close an eye on it.)

For the topping, cut the celeriac into 2cm cubes. Place in a pan, pour on the milk and bring to the boil. Lower the heat and simmer for about 30 minutes until tender. Meanwhile, cut the potatoes into even-sized chunks and boil in salted water for about 15 minutes until tender, then drain well and mash.

Once cooked, drain the celeriac, reserving the milk. Transfer the celeriac to a blender along with half the milk and blitz until smooth. (Or remove about half the milk from the pan and blitz the celeriac in the pan with a stick blender.)

Stir the celeriac into the mashed potato, along with the melted butter and egg yolk. If it looks a little dry, add more of the celeriac cooking milk and season generously with salt and pepper.

Preheat the oven to 200°C/Gas mark 6. Spoon the topping generously over the filling and mark it decoratively with a fork if you like. Bake for about 40 minutes, or until bubbling at the edges and golden on top. Leave the pie to stand for a few minutes before serving.

Game stock

Game stock is particularly rich and tasty. It's always handy to have some in the freezer because it's great for lending a new accent to a dish – even a simple roast chicken can be made to sing when it is served with a gravy made from a stock of wild bird bones. It's a particularly good way of using up the bones and trimmings from your game.

All you need for both light and dark versions is a few simple vegetables and flavourings that you're likely to have to hand, though of course you can add your own embellishments as you go along. You might want to spice it up a little, or add a glut of veg at the same time and pass the whole lot through a sieve to make a quick soup. I don't recommend using liver or heart in stock – they impart a rather unpleasant bitter note. Feel free to chuck in the neck if you like, though.

For delicate dishes a light stock is preferable; for bold, meaty dishes a dark stock works better. The method is much the same, except that for a dark stock the bones and veg are roasted to intensify the flavour. Also, a light stock is cooked more slowly and gently to achieve a crystal-clear result.

This recipe makes a large quantity of stock, but you can scale it down if need be. Alternatively, you could accumulate bones in the freezer until you have enough to make a big batch. You can also reduce your stock down by boiling (to around a quarter of the original volume) after straining – to concentrate the flavour and save space in the freezer. Freeze in small tubs or food bags, adding boiling water to these frozen stock 'bombs' when you want to use them.

Makes about 2 litres

1 large onion
1 carrot
1 celery stick
700g–1kg game bones, either raw
    or cooked (roughly 3 pheasant
    carcasses)

1 bay leaf
A few peppercorns
About 3 litres water

For a light stock

Peel and chop the onion and carrot; chop the celery. Put the vegetables into a large saucepan with all the other ingredients, cover with plenty of cold water and bring slowly to a simmer.

Skim off any scum that forms on the surface, top up again with cold water and return to a simmer. Cook at a low simmer over a gentle heat for a couple of hours.

Taste the stock and, if it is good and flavoursome, remove from the heat. If it still seems a little watery, cook it further to reduce and intensify the flavour. Allow to cool, then pass through a sieve. You can use the stock right away, chill it or freeze it.

For a darker stock
Preheat the oven to 200°C/Gas mark 6.

Wash your onion but keep the skin intact, and roughly chop; peel and roughly chop the carrot; roughly chop the celery. Put these chopped veg along with the game bones into a roasting tray. Roast in the oven for about 30–40 minutes until golden brown.

Now transfer the bones and roasted veg to a saucepan with the other ingredients, cover with cold water and bring to a rolling boil. Skim off any impurities from the surface of the stock and top up with fresh cold water. Simmer rapidly for an hour or two, topping up with water to keep the bones and veg covered as needed. Once you have a nice flavoursome stock, remove from the heat and allow to cool, then pass through a sieve. You can use the stock right away, chill it or freeze it.

Game broth

Simple and tasty, yet elegant enough for the smartest supper table, this is one of those dishes that are good for the soul. Feel free to go as far off-road with it as you like, adding whatever veg you have to hand. Pasta or rice instead of spelt or barley? Go ahead, and add chilli, garlic and/or mushrooms if you like – it's up to you. Just take some stock from the pot, chuck in a handful of pearled spelt or barley and go from there. It's the perfect comforting wintry lunch.

Serves 4

1 litre game stock, light or dark (p.207)
100g pearled spelt or barley
Some leftover cold roast game, chopped, or simply torn apart
½ medium-large leek, shredded and well washed
A few leaves of cavolo nero (or kale or cabbage), well washed, de-stalked and torn into pieces

Sea salt and freshly ground black pepper

To serve
½ small day-old loaf of bread, sliced
1 garlic clove, halved
A little grated Parmesan
Extra virgin olive oil, to drizzle

Preheat the oven to 200°C/Gas mark 6.

Put all the broth ingredients, except the cavolo nero, in a pan, seasoning well with salt and pepper. Bring to a simmer and cook for about 15 minutes until the barley is tender. Check the seasoning, then add the cavolo nero and cook for 2–3 minutes, until it is tender.

Meanwhile, rub the slightly stale bread slices with garlic, sprinkle with Parmesan and revive in the hot oven for a few minutes.

Taste the broth and adjust the seasoning as necessary. Serve topped with a drizzle of good olive oil and accompanied by the hot garlicky bread.

Potted game

This is perfect for those times when you don't have enough of something to make it a meal on its own, or when you want to use up the odds and ends of game in the freezer to free up some space. It also makes a great gift as it keeps very well.

Feel free to chop and change the meat content as much as you like, but do make sure you use enough fat to keep it moist after cooking, and don't skip the seasoning check. It also works well with partridge, mallard, wigeon and wild boar.

Makes about 2 x 500ml jars

1 onion, peeled and roughly chopped
2 garlic cloves, peeled and chopped
600ml medium cider
500ml game stock, light or dark
    (see p.207), or chicken stock will do
A sprig of thyme
500g minced pheasant meat
150g minced bacon
2 points of star anise
6 peppercorns

½ tsp ground mace
50g goose fat
A little oil, for cooking
A couple of bay leaves
Sea salt and freshly ground
    black pepper

Equipment
2 x 500ml hinged ovenproof
    preserving jars, sterilised (see p.216)

Preheat the oven to 120°C/Gas mark ½. Put the onion, garlic, cider and stock into a pan. Add the thyme, bring to the boil and boil hard for about 15 minutes to reduce the liquid down until syrupy. Set aside to cool, then remove the thyme.

Put the minced pheasant and bacon into a large bowl. Crush the star anise and peppercorns using a pestle and mortar and mix with the mace and ½ tsp salt. Add to the bacon and pheasant, then add the goose fat. Mix in the reduced liquor. To test the seasoning, fry a little piece of the mixture in a little oil for a minute or two, then taste. Adjust the seasoning of the main mix accordingly, re-testing if need be.

Pack the mixture into the preserving jars and place a bay leaf on top of each. Place the jars, still open, in a roasting tray and pour enough hot water into the tray to come about 3cm up the sides of the jars. Place in the oven for 1½ hours.

Remove the jars from the water bath and close the lids while they are still hot to create a vacuum in the jar as the contents cool.

When cooled, these jars of potted game will keep in the fridge unopened for up to 2 weeks. Once opened, use within a few days. Delicious with sourdough toast and pickled cucumbers or green sauce (p.244), and an extra sprinkling of pepper.

Game rillettes

A classic dish from the Alsace region of northern France, rillettes was developed as a way to preserve meat for the leaner months. It is essentially a form of confit, usually made with farmed duck legs, which are cooked slowly in fat, then stored in the same fat. I like to use the legs of wild duck, pheasant or rabbit, or indeed a mixture of them all.

To get the best flavour, it's important to cure the meats lightly first; this also helps to preserve the meat. You will need to assess how much cure you need to make. One batch, as described below, will cure about 500g meat. Err on the side of generosity. You want enough cure to season all the meat liberally and, if you make too much, you can always use it up at a later date. This recipe works with mallard, rabbit, pheasant, hare, or even grouse or wild boar.

Makes about 2 x 500ml jars

500g game meat: wild duck legs
    (skin on or off), rabbit haunches,
    pheasant legs or hare shoulders
    on the bone
1 onion, peeled and quartered
1 garlic bulb, halved horizontally
About 850ml duck fat or vegetable oil
    (depending on the chosen game
    and size of your cooking vessel)
Ground mace, to taste
Sea salt and freshly ground
    black pepper

For the cure
4 peppercorns
1 point from a star anise
2 tsp table salt
2 tsp light brown sugar
2 bay leaves, shredded
A little grated orange zest
A sprig of rosemary, chopped
A sprig of thyme, chopped

Equipment
2 x 500ml hinged preserving jars, or a
    1-litre loaf tin lined with cling film

For the cure, crush the spices and combine with the salt, sugar and shredded bay leaves. Add the orange zest and finely chopped rosemary and thyme.

Put your meat into a ceramic, plastic or stainless-steel dish and rub the cure well into the pieces, using all of it. Leave in the fridge for at least 2 hours, preferably overnight.

Rinse off the cure from the meat under cold running water. Place the meat in a saucepan (large enough to contain it all), with the onion and garlic. If you are using duck fat, warm it gently until liquid. Pour enough duck fat or vegetable oil over the meat to just cover it.

Place on a low heat until the fat is just simmering, then allow it to cook at the slowest possible simmer, without a lid, until tender. This may take over 2 hours.

Meanwhile, sterilise your jars: wash them thoroughly then place on a tray in a low oven (120°C/Gas mark ½), for around 15 minutes with the lids open.

Once the meat is tender enough to fall from the bone, remove from the heat and allow to cool for an hour or so.

Now carefully pour the contents of the pan into a colander over a large bowl. Once the fat and juices have strained through, place the meat back in the same pan. Separate the fat and liquid in the bowl by skimming the fat from the top of the liquid, using a ladle, into a separate bowl. (Alternatively, if you're using duck fat, you could put the bowl in the fridge once it has cooled and wait for the fat to set before draining off the liquid or scraping off the fat. Once removed, you will need to melt the fat so it is ready to use.) Set both fat and liquid aside.

Take the meat off the bones and place it, along with the reserved cooking liquid (not the fat), in a food mixer or large bowl. Mix or beat well with a wooden spoon, adding the reserved fat, about half a ladle at a time, and seasoning with mace, salt and pepper to taste as you go. If you like, you can incorporate the soft flesh from the cooked garlic as well. The secret here is to add enough fat to give a good balance: too fatty and the rillettes will be unpleasantly greasy; too little and the dish will be dry. If the mixture seems to start to split or separate, stop adding fat immediately. You may be surprised by how much fat the meat will hold. It's also helpful to remember that the fat is there to serve more than one purpose – as well as being tasty it will keep the air from your rillettes, prolonging the shelf life.

Check the seasoning, remembering that the rillettes will be served cold, and you therefore need to be a little more generous. When you are happy with the consistency and taste, pack the mixture into the warm sterilised glass jars, seal and leave to cool. Once cooled, store in the fridge for up to 4 weeks. Once opened, keep refrigerated and use within a few days.

Drake's drop,
a cold day tipple

This recipe is a variation on bullshot, which is a cross between beef consommé and a Bloody Mary. I created it for a friend's shoot-day elevenses, for two reasons. Firstly, because I didn't have any beef bones to make a beef stock and secondly, because the shoot involved a very challenging duck drive with birds flying at colossal heights, making it hard indeed to drop a duck or drake from the sky. I like a pun. It's sad, I know, but I can't help it.

The key to this recipe is creating an intensely flavoured stock. I add roasted duck carcasses to a prepared dark game stock for a strong and savoury duck flavour that is full of vigour.

Serves 8 or more

2 duck carcasses
1 litre dark game stock (see p.207)
1 litre good-quality tomato juice

Tabasco and Worcestershire sauce,
   to taste
Vodka, to finish

Preheat the oven to 180°C/Gas mark 4. Place the duck carcasses in a roasting tin in the oven for about 20 minutes.

Transfer the roasted carcasses to a saucepan that will hold them both and cover with the game stock, topping up at this point with water if necessary (but not later if it starts to reduce a little because you want a nice intense stock). Simmer for an hour or so and then take off the heat and leave to cool before removing the carcasses. Pass through a sieve and reserve.

Heat the stock and tomato juice to a gentle simmer and turn off the heat. Season with Tabasco and Worcestershire sauce. Ladle into cups and top off with a little vodka to keep out the cold.

Venison carpaccio

I suppose this dish really ought to be done with Chinese water deer, but it works very well with all venison meat and I have, on occasion, made it with pigeon and even duck breasts. The Asian flavours give a different dimension to the classic Italian version flavoured with Parmesan, lemon and olive oil.

Serves 4

350g piece of loin or seamed-out haunch of venison (very fresh)
50ml rapeseed oil, plus extra to rub into the meat
1 garlic clove, peeled and very finely chopped
½ medium-hot red chilli
5mm piece of fresh root ginger, peeled and very finely chopped
50ml good dark soy sauce
25ml toasted sesame oil

Juice of 1 lime
3 or 4 green cabbage leaves
Sea salt and freshly ground black pepper

To garnish
3 spring onions (green and white parts), thinly sliced
A few sprigs of coriander
50g sesame seeds, toasted in a dry pan until fragrant then cooled

Place a heavy-based frying pan over a high heat. Rub the venison all over with rapeseed oil and season with a little salt and pepper. When the pan is very hot, add the piece of venison and fry for only a few seconds on all sides – to just colour the outside of the meat. (You are not trying to cook the venison, just adding another layer of flavour and killing off any bacteria on the surface of the meat to make extra sure it's safe to eat raw.)

In a small bowl, combine the garlic, chilli, ginger, soy sauce, rapeseed oil and sesame oil to make a dressing.

Cut the venison into slices the thickness of a £1 coin, ensuring you slice against the grain of the meat. Arrange the slices overlapping on a serving platter large enough to hold them all comfortably without piling them up. Spoon a little of the dressing over the venison slices and sprinkle with the lime juice.

Shred the cabbage leaves as finely as you can. Dress these with a little more of the dressing and scatter over and around the venison. Garnish with the spring onions and coriander and sprinkle over the toasted sesame seeds. Serve immediately.

Venison with marrow pickle

A seamed-out venison haunch will provide you with plenty of steak-quality meat. It's nice served with a little pickle, as it cuts the richness of the meat beautifully. I sometimes make the pickle into a ketchup by blending it and cooking it a little more, then serving the thinly cut steaks smeared with the ketchup in a bread roll as a sort of burger. The steak and pickle version has a touch more class, though.

Serves 4

For the marrow pickle
A good chunk of marrow, about 250g
1 tsp sea salt
1 tsp ground turmeric
1 tsp coriander seeds
½ tsp cumin seeds
200ml cider vinegar
125g golden caster sugar
A good sprig of dill

For the steaks
4 venison steaks, about 200g each
Sunflower oil, for cooking
About 100g butter
A few thyme sprigs
Sea salt and freshly ground black pepper

Equipment
A 350ml pickle jar, sterilised (see p.216)

Make the pickle well ahead. Cut the marrow into quarters lengthways, scrape out the soft pulpy seeds using a spoon, then cut into slices the thickness of a £1 coin. Toss in a bowl with the salt, then leave for 10 minutes to let the salt draw out water from the marrow. Squeeze in a tea towel to remove more water; discard the liquid.

Put the spices, vinegar and sugar in a pan over a medium-low heat and stir until the sugar has dissolved, then simmer until reduced by a third. Add the marrow and cook until tender but still crunchy, about 10 minutes. Put into the sterilised jar with the dill and seal. Once cooled, this pickle will keep in the fridge for a few weeks.

Have your venison steaks at room temperature when ready to cook them. Heat a frying pan over a medium-high heat. Season the steaks and rub generously with oil. Add the steaks to the hot pan with a knob of butter and cook for 2–3 minutes until golden brown and rich on the underside, then turn them over. Don't move the steaks in the pan until you turn them. As you flip them, add more butter to the pan, along with the thyme (as the steaks have little fat of their own, you need a fair amount of butter). Cook for a further 2–3 minutes, depending on thickness and preference for medium or medium-rare (they'll continue to cook as they rest).

Rest the steaks in a warm place for at least as long as they have been cooked. Serve them with the pickle and maybe a few chips.

Herb marinade
with star anise

This is a useful little flavour enhancer and a great way to keep game in the fridge in a state of readiness for all sorts of different recipes. You can use other woody (or 'hard') herbs such as marjoram or savory in place of the rosemary or thyme.

You can rub this mix on venison a day or two before cooking, but it will do the job in just a few minutes if need be. It's also great for wild duck, rabbit or pheasant. It's a good barbecue marinade too.

Makes 50ml

1 star anise
7 black peppercorns
A sprig of thyme

A sprig of rosemary
1 tsp salt
50ml rapeseed oil

Crush the star anise and peppercorns together using a pestle and mortar or a spice grinder. Don't worry about making it too fine – a little character is a good thing. Remove your thyme and rosemary leaves from the stems and chop them. Add these to the spices and salt and bash a little more.

Add the oil and the marinade is ready. You can rub it straight away on to the meat you're using, or keep it in the fridge for a week. If you're not cooking the meat that day, this marinade really helps to keep the meat in good condition in the fridge. There's no need to wash it off before cooking.

Venison liver persillade

For this French dish, fresh liver is lightly sautéed, then dressed with a shallot and parsley salad spiked with capers and finished with a warm sauce made from the cooking butter and a little stock and vinegar. It's usually done with calves' liver, but works very well – if not a little better – with very fresh venison liver.

Serves 2

4 generous but thin slices of venison
   liver, around 8mm thick,
   larger tubes removed
A handful of plain flour, well seasoned
A knob of butter
A sprig of parsley, roughly chopped
1 tsp baby capers

1 shallot, peeled and very finely sliced
A dash of good balsamic vinegar
About 120ml light game stock
   (p.207) or venison stock, or
   chicken stock will do
Sea salt and freshly ground
   black pepper

Place a large frying pan over a medium-high heat. Dust your liver slices in the seasoned flour and pop them in the hot pan with half the butter. Cook quickly for around 2 minutes on each side, so the outside is brown and the inside is nice and moist, even a little pink if you like it that way. Feel the liver carefully with a finger – it will firm up a little when it's ready.

Place the liver on a warm plate and scatter over the chopped parsley, capers and shallot. Add the rest of the butter to the pan, still on the heat, and wait until it stops bubbling, then pour it over the liver. The parsley should crackle as the butter softens it. Set aside in a warm spot while you make the sauce.

Add a dash of balsamic vinegar to the pan and return it to the heat, then add the stock and let this bubble in the pan for a minute or two until reduced to a rich sauce. Add the resting juices from the liver, then pour the sauce back over the whole thing. Serve with plenty of mashed potato and a nice bottle of red.

Wild boar Holstein

Originating from the region of northern Germany of the same name, this simple, quick and tasty dish is usually made with veal. The crunch of the breadcrumbs and the way the meat semi-steams inside the coating marry with the flavour of the boar and the salty anchovies to yield lip-smacking results. The recipe also works well with venison.

Serves 2

2 wild boar escalopes (from the seamed-out haunch or the loin)
A good handful of plain white flour, well seasoned
3 free-range eggs
50g breadcrumbs
A couple of knobs of butter

1 tsp small capers (less if you're using stronger, bigger ones)
A couple of sprigs of parsley, leaves only, chopped
A few anchovy fillets, sliced lengthways
Sea salt and freshly ground black pepper

Trim the thin, steak-like escalopes of any sinew and then gently flatten them using a rolling pin between two sheets of cling film. Don't get carried away and make them too thin or they will become too fragile to handle.

Put the seasoned flour into a dish. In a second dish, beat one of the eggs with a little water. Put the breadcrumbs into a third dish. Dust the boar escalopes in the seasoned flour, then dip into the beaten egg. Finally place in the breadcrumbs and turn to coat them evenly all over.

Heat a frying pan over a medium heat. Add a knob of butter, then the escalopes. Cook for a couple of minutes until nicely golden brown underneath, then turn the meat over and cook the other side for a couple of minutes. Remove the meat to a warmed plate.

Add a little more butter to the pan and gently fry the remaining 2 eggs to your liking. When they are just about done, remove the pan from the heat and add the capers and chopped parsley to warm through.

Transfer the escalopes to warmed serving plates and place a fried egg on each one. Top with the anchovies and dress with the warm caper and parsley butter.

Roasted squirrels

The autumn, when this year's brood of grey squirrels are starting to fatten up for the long cold winter, is the best time to cook this recipe. A young squirrel born earlier in the year is perfect for roasting very simply in this way; do not try this with an older squirrel.

Serves 3

3 fully grown but young squirrels, skinned and gutted, heads, tails and feet removed
Olive oil, for cooking
1 garlic bulb, halved horizontally
A few bay leaves

1 lemon
1 tsp coriander seeds
A sprig of rosemary, leaves only, finely chopped
Sea salt and freshly ground black pepper

Preheat the oven to 200°C/Gas mark 6. Make sure the squirrels are at room temperature before you roast them and dry them off with a clean tea towel or kitchen paper if necessary. Add a little oil to a large non-stick roasting tray and place in the hot oven for 3–4 minutes until the oil is nice and hot but not smoking.

Rub the squirrels all over with olive oil and season well with salt and pepper. Carefully place the squirrels in the roasting tray, add the garlic and bay leaves and roast in the oven for 5 minutes. Take the tray out of the oven, squeeze half the lemon juice over the squirrels and add the coriander and rosemary. Drop the spent lemon half into the tray and return to the oven for 5 minutes, then turn off the oven but leave the tray of squirrels inside for a further 3–4 minutes.

Remove the tray from the oven and lift the squirrels on to a warmed serving platter. Pour over the juices from the tray, drizzle with more olive oil, sprinkle with a little more salt and finally squeeze over the juice from the other lemon half. Serve the squirrels with a simple salad and some nice crusty bread.

Hare blood cake

This is basically a small but very tasty black pudding, cooked in a dish in the oven rather than in a sausage skin. Traditionally, hare blood is used to season and thicken a stew known as 'jugged hare' but I think this is a better use for it.

Serves 6–8, as a starter or light lunch

A good knob of butter (or duck fat)
1 small onion, peeled and
    finely chopped
2 garlic cloves, peeled and
    finely chopped
1 tsp chopped thyme leaves
¼ tsp ground allspice
¼ tsp chilli flakes
½ tsp smoked paprika

250ml very fresh hare blood (i.e. from
    2–3 hares), sieved
75g oatmeal (ideally pinhead)
A shot of good-quality malt whisky
100g pork back fat, cut into 5mm dice
Sea salt and freshly ground black
    pepper

Equipment
A 500g loaf tin or ceramic baking dish

Preheat the oven to 100°C/Gas mark ¼. Line a small loaf tin or ceramic baking dish with a double layer of cling film, leaving enough overhanging the sides to fold over the top.

Heat the butter in a pan large enough to hold all the ingredients. Add the onion, garlic, thyme and spices and sweat gently until soft, about 10 minutes.

Add the hare blood, oatmeal and whisky to the pan. Continue to cook over a low heat until the mixture thickens (it needs to be thick enough to hold the pork fat in suspension). As soon as it reaches this stage, take off the heat and add the pork fat.

Now you need to check the seasoning. I often just taste the mixture as it is, but if that's too vampire-esque for you, cook off a spoonful in a small hot pan and taste that. Adjust the seasoning of the mixture accordingly.

Pour the mixture into the prepared tin or dish and fold the overhanging cling film over the top. Stand the container in a roasting tray containing enough warm water to come halfway up the sides. Cook in the oven for 45 minutes or until set firm.

Remove from the tray of water and set aside to cool. You can then fry off slices of the blood cake and serve them on toast, or use in any other way that you would black pudding (bearing in mind that this hare version has a stronger flavour). Keep refrigerated until needed and use within a week, or freeze for later use.

Roast saddle of hare
with bay and sumac

This is based on a barbecued rabbit dish I first tried in Morocco. I think it works just as well in the oven with hare, though I also do it – with rabbit or hare – on the barbecue and serve it with freshly made flat breads. Sumac is a strangely smoky, citrus-zingy crushed berry from the Middle East, which you will find in good delis and supermarkets. This is also a good way to cook muntjac and other venison.

Serves 2

1 hare saddle, belly meat and ribs trimmed back to the edge of the 'eye' meat
A little extra virgin rapeseed oil, for cooking
6 bay leaves
A glug of good extra virgin olive oil, to drizzle

2 garlic cloves, peeled and finely chopped
About ½ tsp ground sumac
½ lemon
Sea salt and freshly ground black pepper

Preheat the oven to 200°C/Gas mark 6. Season the saddle of hare with salt and pepper and rub it with a little rapeseed oil. Heat a heavy-based ovenproof frying pan until it's good and hot. Place your bay leaves in the pan and then add the hare saddle. Cook for around 4 minutes, allowing the meat and leaves to char slightly, turning the meat a few times.

Trickle over a little more rapeseed oil and transfer the pan to the oven. Roast for 8–10 minutes, or until the meat is cooked and feels firmish. Take the hare from the oven and allow it to rest in the pan for at least 5 minutes, but not longer than 15 minutes. Meanwhile, mix the extra virgin olive oil with the garlic.

Carve the meat lengthways from the bone to give you the two loins, then slice into three pieces. Arrange on a serving plate and drizzle with the garlicky olive oil. Sprinkle with the sumac and squeeze over a little lemon juice.

A good accompaniment to this dish is the Middle Eastern spiced potato dish batata harra, or you can serve it with couscous. You can also cut the hare meat into chunks to serve as a canapé.

Potted hare

This is similar to rillettes (p.215) but done in a very old English fashion. I think it's delicious and a fine way to use up the shoulder meat of a hare, which can otherwise be a bit stringy. It also works with rabbit and pheasant.

Makes a 500ml jar, serves 6 as a starter

6 hare shoulders, or 2 shoulders and
    2 legs on the bone
1kg unsalted butter
1 garlic bulb, halved horizontally
A sprig of rosemary
A glass of good red wine
Sea salt, freshly ground black pepper
    and ground mace

For the marinade
2 juniper berries
½ star anise
6 bay leaves
6 white peppercorns
1 heaped tsp coarse sea salt

To serve
Warm toast
Quick pickled onions
    (see overleaf), or other
    crunchy pickle

Equipment
500ml Kilner jar, sterilised
    (see p.216), or a ceramic dish
    or pot

For the marinade, roughly bash all the spices together with the salt. Put the meat into a dish and rub it liberally with the dry spice mixture. Leave to marinate in the fridge for at least 24 hours, but no longer than 48 hours.

Preheat the oven to 180°C/Gas mark 4. Melt the butter slowly in a small pan over a low heat.

Place the hare meat in a casserole dish or roasting tray in which it fits snugly. Add the garlic bulb and rosemary.

Pour over the butter and then the wine. If necessary add a little water, so the hare is more or less submerged. Cover the dish and cook in the oven for about 3 hours until the hare meat is very tender and just falling off the bone. Leave immersed in the butter to cool to room temperature.

Once cooled, carefully pour the contents of the pan into a colander placed over a large bowl. Allow the fat and juices to strain through, then remove the meat from the bones.

Separate the butter and liquid by skimming the butter from the top of the liquid, using a ladle, into a separate bowl. (Alternatively, you could put the bowl in the fridge once it has cooled and wait for the butter to set before taking it off the liquid. Once removed, you will need to melt the butter, so it is ready to use). Set both fat and liquid aside.

Place the meat in a food mixer or large bowl and add the reserved cooking liquid (not the butter), making sure the liquid is no more than half the volume of the meat. Mix or beat well with a wooden spoon, adding as much of the reserved melted butter as the mixture will take without becoming greasy, about half a ladleful at a time. Season with mace, salt and pepper to taste as you go, remembering that it is to be served cold, so you may need to be generous with the salt and pepper. Place in a sterilised jar or ceramic dish and smooth the surface. Pour over a final, thin layer of the butter and, once cool, refrigerate.

Serve your potted hare as a starter or lunch, with good toast and some quick pickled onions or another tart, crunchy pickle. Alternatively, it works very well stirred into piping-hot pasta with a few dried chilli flakes and some chopped parsley. Save any butter left from cooking the hare – it's great on toast in its own right, or used to dress some nice vegetables.

Quick pickled onions Slice your onions evenly, but not too thinly, and season well with salt, sugar and black pepper. Leave in a glass or china bowl for a few minutes to allow the salt and sugar to draw out some of the juices and soften the onions. Pour off the excess liquid, then sprinkle with plenty of good cider vinegar. If you like, you can embellish the onions with a few chopped chives. In the fridge, they will keep for a week or so.

Tuscan rabbit livers

This quick, cheaty dish is a winner. It comes, unsurprisingly, from the Italian region of Tuscany. Rabbit livers are strong in flavour, so you need plenty of garlic and tomatoes to stand up to them. Only use very fresh, healthy-looking rabbit livers for this – or any other dish for that matter. You can prepare this recipe in advance if you like, but not too far ahead; it is best eaten warm and is never the same once it's been in the fridge.

Serves 2 or 4 (depending on appetite)

3 very ripe tomatoes, or 12 very ripe cherry tomatoes
4 garlic cloves, peeled
A glug of very good extra virgin olive oil
A few basil leaves, torn
Livers from 6 rabbits, cut in half, trimmed and cleaned

A knob of butter
A glug of Marsala wine (or medium sherry, such as a good solera)
A few slices of good sourdough bread
Sea salt and freshly ground black pepper

Cut the tomatoes into small pieces, or quarters if using cherry tomatoes. Place them in a bowl and season with salt and pepper. Finely slice one of the garlic cloves and add to the tomatoes with a glug of very good olive oil and some torn basil. Set aside to macerate.

Place a non-stick pan, large enough to hold all the livers, over a medium heat. Season the livers well with salt and pepper. When the pan is hot, add a little butter, then add the livers and cook for a minute or so but don't move them about.

Now turn all the rabbit livers over and add a little more butter, if needed, along with 2 finely chopped garlic cloves. Add the Marsala (carefully, as it may ignite). Cook over a high heat until the liquid has mostly evaporated and then turn off the heat. The whole cooking process won't take more than a few minutes. Be sure not to overcook the livers or they will be a bit dry.

Allow to cool a little, then break up the livers with the back of a fork or pop them in a blender and pulse to a coarse texture.

Toast your bread and halve the final garlic clove. Rub both sides of the toast with the cut surface of the garlic. Spread the livers on the warm toast and spoon on the tomatoes. Finish with more freshly torn basil.

Game curry

Some years ago, I was involved in a River Cottage quest to get the country eating more wild rabbit. Along the way, I got the chance to cook in the kitchen of a local curry house with a wonderful, if slightly intimidating lady called Helen. She set me straight on a few things to do with curry cooking. This aromatic, spicy curry is basically her recipe with a few twists of my own (thank you, Helen). It also works well with pheasant, grouse, pigeon, goose, hare, squirrel and wild boar.

Serves 4–6

3 tbsp sunflower or rapeseed oil
1 cinnamon stick, broken in half
4 cardamom pods
1 bay leaf
2 large onions, peeled and chopped
2 tbsp garlic and ginger paste (see below)
1 tsp each ground cumin, coriander, turmeric, paprika and chilli powder
2 tinned peeled plum tomatoes (or skinned fresh tomatoes)
2 tsp nigella (black onion) seeds

2 rabbits, jointed into 8 pieces each, scored, bones in
1 tsp garam masala
Sea salt and freshly ground black pepper

To finish

Red pepper and fresh root ginger julienne (thin strips), or coriander leaves

Heat the oil in a large pan over a medium heat. Add the cinnamon, cardamom pods and bay leaf and fry for a minute. Add the onions and the garlic and ginger paste, with a good pinch of salt, and sweat gently for about 10 minutes, until soft. Add all the other ground spices, except the garam masala, and cook for a few minutes until the oil separates from the spices and they release their aroma.

Squash the tomatoes to a pulp in your hands, or crush with a fork, and add to the pan, along with the black onion seeds. Add the rabbit and enough water just to cover the meat. Bring to a simmer, turn the heat down low and put a lid on the pan. Cook gently for about 45 minutes or until the rabbit is tender, stirring often.

Stir in the garam masala and check the seasoning, adding more salt and pepper if needed. Serve scattered with red pepper and ginger julienne or coriander leaves.

P.S. To make a ginger and garlic paste, blitz 50g each of peeled garlic cloves and fresh root ginger and 85ml water in a food processor, or chop the garlic and ginger and pound with a pestle and mortar before stirring in the water. You'll have more than you need for this recipe; refrigerate the rest in a jar and use within a week.

Hot-smoked rabbit saddle

This wonderful dish will convert even steadfast non-rabbit eaters to the cause, especially if you top it off with a little green sauce (see p.244). The only item of equipment you need is a simple hot smoker. It's a good idea to smoke 4–6 saddles at the same time. Once cooled, they can be frozen for later use if required. This recipe also works well with saddles of hare.

Serves 4–6

4 rabbit saddles, well trimmed
About 30g butter
2 bay leaves

For the cure
2 peppercorns, crushed
1 bay leaf, chopped
1 point from a star anise, crushed
2 tsp light brown sugar
2 tsp table salt

To serve
Green sauce (p.244)

Equipment
Hot smoker (see p.200)
Wood shavings

Lay the rabbit saddles in a deep dish. Mix all the cure ingredients together and sprinkle evenly all over the rabbit. Leave to cure for around 15 minutes, turning occasionally.

Rinse the cure off the saddles and pat them dry. Now, set up your smoker and get the smoke going. Place the saddles inside and smoke for 6–7 minutes, depending on how hot your smoker is. You are not trying to cook the rabbit meat through, just flavour it with smokiness.

Place a heavy-based frying pan over a medium heat and add the butter. Once it is foaming, add the bay leaves and rabbit saddles. Cook slowly, turning every few minutes, until the rabbit is firm to the touch – around 8 minutes should do it, less for a smaller rabbit. Turn off the heat and let the rabbit rest in the hot pan for about 10 minutes; this will allow the inside to just cook through. Don't overcook the rabbit or it will be dry.

To serve, remove the loins from the bone, saving the bones for stock, and cut into bite-sized pieces. Serve on a board, with green sauce for dipping, as a canapé. Alternatively, you could turn it into a supper with the addition of mash and carrots.

Green sauce

I first came across this vibrant little beauty while working for the amazing Fergus Henderson at St John Bar and Restaurant in London. It was paired with hot roasted mutton, stuffed into buns. I was instantly hooked and it is seldom off the menu in my house. It's the perfect accompaniment to all strong-flavoured meats, hot or cold.

You can use whatever soft, leafy herbs you like. It works well in different seasons – basil in the summer, marjoram and thyme in the winter – but I always include mint and parsley in the mix.

Makes a small jar

A bunch of flat-leaf or curly parsley (about 50g)
A small bunch of mint (about 25g)
A small bunch of basil, tarragon, broad-leaved thyme or marjoram (about 25g)
2 tsp mustard (preferably Dijon)
1½ tbsp cider vinegar or red wine vinegar
A large garlic clove, peeled and finely chopped

2 tsp tiny capers
4 anchovy fillets, roughly chopped
A couple of good glugs of very good olive or rapeseed oil

Equipment
A small Kilner jar or jam jar, sterilised (see p.216)

Wash, dry and chop your herbs well, but not too finely, using a sharp knife so you don't end up with the texture of grass cuttings.

Place the chopped herbs in a bowl with all the other ingredients, except the oil. Mix together and then work in enough oil to give a relish consistency.

Pour the green sauce into your sterilised jar. Pour a thin layer of oil over the surface to protect the sauce from the air and seal with the lid. It will then keep in the fridge for about 4 days.

Useful Things

Directory

The British Association for Shooting & Conservation (BASC)
basc.org.uk
All the information you could possibly need on shooting, from firearms safety to species identification. BASC also runs courses on everything from gun safety to pest control management.

Game & Wildlife Conservation Trust (GWCT)
gwct.org.uk
Pioneers in wildlife conservation, this research body is improving our knowledge of game and understanding of our interaction with the natural world to keep a sustainable check on shooting practices.

The National Gamekeepers Organisation (NGO)
nationalgamekeepers.org.uk
For all things gamekeeping related, NGO aims to ensure high standards throughout the profession.

The British Deer Society (BDS)
bds.org.uk
Highly committed group of deer enthusiasts, who carry out studies of deer numbers, habitats and activities. A reliable source of information.

Royal Society for the Protection of Birds (RSPB)
rspb.org.uk
For further information on bird species, including recognition guides.

British Trust for Ornithology (BTO)
bto.org
Independent charitable research institute, which monitors wildlife populations, especially birds, across the UK, to advise on conservation.

Countryside Alliance (CA)
countryside-alliance.org
Along with BASC and GWCT, the CA is working hard to promote the use of more game meat in the UK. Check their game-to-eat page for advice on local game suppliers and game events across the country.

Taste of Game
tasteofgame.org.uk
A national notice board for game food events, game suppliers and recipes.

Food Standards Agency (FSA)
food.gov.uk
Provides useful advice on safe food-handling procedures, including a download on game handling.

Specialist game dealers

Gourmet Game
01205 724274

La Chasse
lachasselimited.co.uk

Mid Shires Foods Ltd
midshiresfoods.co.uk

Specialist courses

The BASC, GWCT, BDS and FSA (see left) run training courses on everything from hunting to safe meat handling. For courses on learning how to shoot, prepare and cook your own game, I can recommend the following:

Vale House Kitchen
valehousekitchen.co.uk

Seasoned Cookery School
seasonedcourses.com

River Cottage
rivercottage.net

Butchery equipment and cookware

Pro Cook
procook.co.uk

Smiths
awsmith.co.uk

Weschenfelder
weschenfelder.co.uk
For sausage-making equipment, in particular.

Further reading

Deer Watch: A Field Guide
by Richard Prior
An invaluable field guide to the different species of deer in the UK.

Will's Pigeon Shooting
by Will Garfit
Excellent guide to shooting wood pigeons from an expert.

The Book of the Woodcock
by Colin Laurie McElvie
Fully illustrated game shooter's guide, the first of its kind on this bird.

The Wildfowler
by H C Folkard
Must-have guide for any serious wildfowl hunter.

A Natural History of the Pheasant
by Peter Robertson
Detailed account of the pheasant's life and habitat.

Training Manual for Deer Stalkers
by The British Deer Society
Excellent technical reference guide.

Acknowledgements

Thanks to the River Cottage gang: Hugh Fearnley-Whittingstall, Rob Love, Steve Lamb, Gill Meller, John Wright and Lucy Brazier; thanks especially to Nikki Duffy for making me do it properly.

To the very talented Bloomsbury bunch: Natalie Bellos, Xa Shaw Stewart, Alison Glossop and Ellen Williams. Thanks also to the rest of the handbook creative team: Janet Illsley, Will Webb and his dog, Gavin Kingcome and Toby Atkins.

To the friends: Mark Diacono, Robin Rea, Rupert and Clare Major, Daniel Howe, Duncan Thomas, Bod and Annie Griffiths, James Fitzharris, Adam Franklin, Dale Johnson, John Penny, David and Karen Richards, James Yarrow, Will Garfit, Simon and Selina Barr, Steve Colmer, Ant Brown, Andrew Vernon, Nigel Partis, Frank Shellard, Nick Assirati, Hazel Paterson and Jonathan McGee. Special thanks go to Brendan Buesnel for some deft camera work and for just being one of the good guys.

And to the family: Abi and Gavin Atterton, Mum and Dad, and Peter Bird Pickford. Special mention must go to Caroline Maddams for putting up with my endless 'research' trips.

Photography credits

Index

Page numbers in *italic* refer to the illustrations